Anne Frank's Diary

Anne Frank's Diary

The Graphic Adaptation

Anne Frank

Adapted by Ari Folman
Illustrations by David Polonsky

PANTHEON BOOKS, NEW YORK

Library of Congress Cataloging-in-Publication Data
Names: Frank, Anne. Polonsky, David, illustrator. Folman, Ari, editor.
Title: Anne Frank's diary : the graphic adaptation / Anne Frank ; illustrations by David Polonsky ; adapted by Ari Folman.
Description: First edition. New York : Pantheon Books, 2018
Identifiers: LCCN 2017034415. ISBN 9781101871799 (hardcover : alk. paper). ISBN 9781101871805 (ebook).
Subjects: LCSH: Frank, Anne, 1929-1945—Comic books, strips, etc. Jewish children in the Holocaust—Netherlands—Amsterdam—Biography—Comic books, strips, etc. Jews—Persecutions—Netherlands—Amsterdam—Biography—Comic books, strips, etc. Amsterdam (Netherlands)—Biography—Comic books, strips, etc.
Classification: LCC DS135.N6 F731865 2018. DDC 940.53/18092 [B]—dc23.
LC record available at lccn.loc.gov/2017034415

www.pantheonbooks.com

Printed in China
First Edition
4 6 8 9 7 5 3

Cast of Characters

The Frank Family

Anne Frank

Margot Frank
Anne's sister (three years older)

Otto Frank ("Pim")
Anne's father

Edith Frank
Anne's mother

The Other Residents
(Real names are in brackets)

Peter van Daan
[Peter van Pels]

Petronella van Daan ("Madame")
[Auguste van Pels]
Peter's mother

Hermann van Daan
[Hermann van Pels]
Peter's father

Albert Dussel (the dentist)
[Fritz Pfeffer]

The Helpers

Johannes (Jo) Kleiman
An accountant at
Opekta and Pectacon,
Otto Frank's companies

Victor Kugler
An Opekta employee

Bep Voskuijl
A secretary at Opekta
and the daughter
of employee Johan Voskuijl

Miep Gies
Otto Frank's secretary

Jan Gies
Miep's husband

Johan Voskuijl
Bep's father and the
warehouse manager at Opekta

Anne Frank's Diary

Friday, June 12–Saturday, June 20, 1942

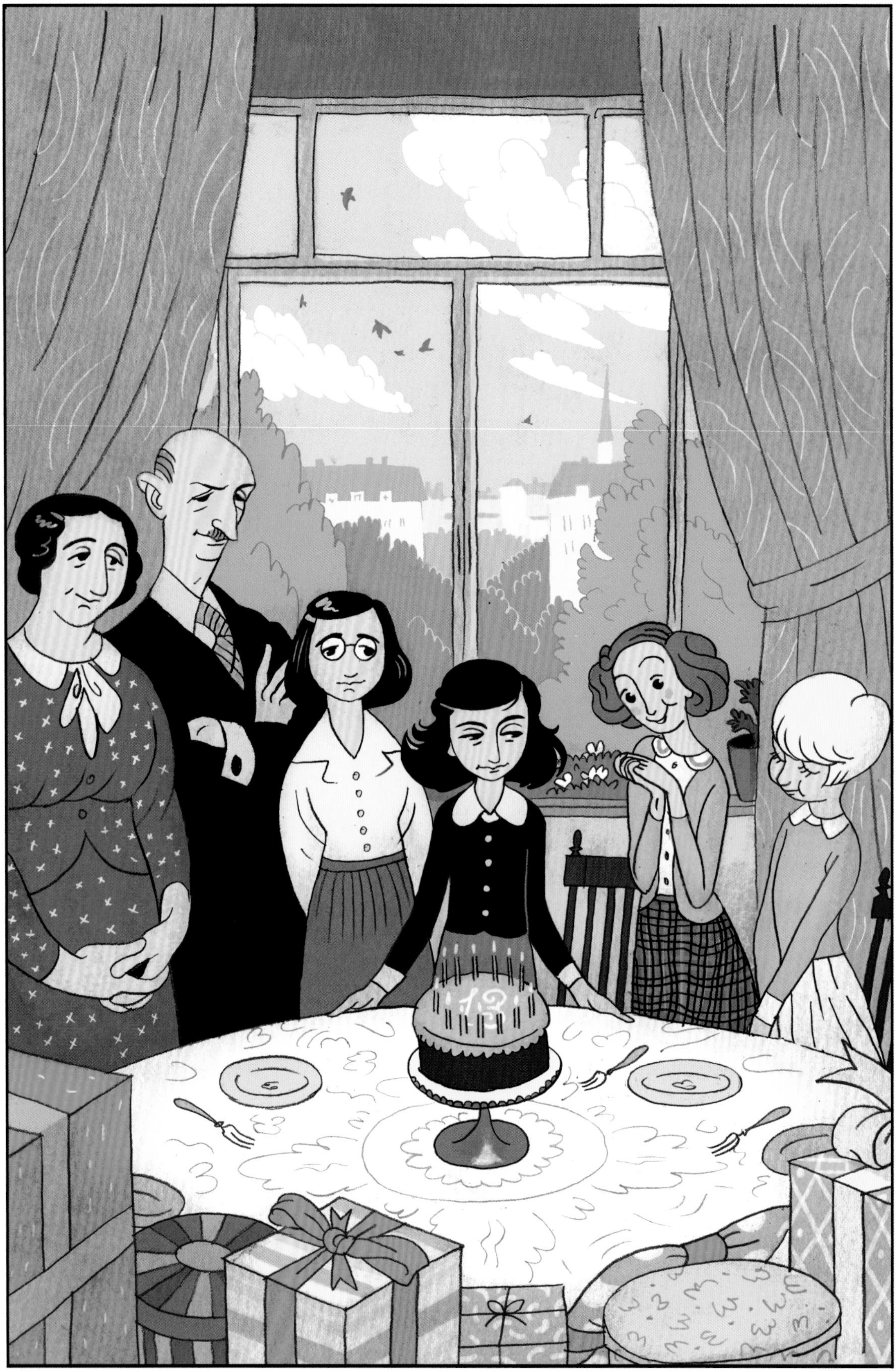

No one would believe me, but at the age of 13, I feel totally alone in this world.

I have loving parents and a 16-year-old sister.

WHAT ARE YOU WAITING FOR, ANNE? COME AND OPEN YOUR PRESENTS!

Hanneli and Jacqueline are supposedly my best friends, but I've never had a real friend.

SHE DOES LIKE TO BE THE CENTER OF ATTENTION, DOESN'T SHE?

I have a throng of admirers who can't keep their adoring eyes off me.

ANNE! COME DOWN! I CAN'T LIVE WITHOUT YOU!

ROB, GO HOME!! I SWEAR I'M GOING TO CALL THE POLICE!

All I think about when I'm with friends is having a good time. I can't bring myself to talk about anything but ordinary everyday things.

Much as I try, I can't get any closer to people. That is why...

...as soon as I saw you among my other presents...

I knew you were special!

So you are going to be the closest friend I never had in my life...

...and I'm going to call this friend Kitty.

Dear Kitty, I hope I will be able to confide everything to you, as I have never been able to confide in anyone, and I hope you will be a great source of comfort and support.

I'd better provide a brief sketch of my life. My father and mother married in Germany, in 1925. It was not love at first sight...

DOES IT BOTHER YOU THAT I AM MUCH OLDER?

HOW WOULD I KNOW... YOU'RE MY FIRST ONE.

My sister, Margot, was born in 1926.

ISN'T SHE THE PRETTIEST BABY EVER?

YOU SHOULDN'T SAY THAT, DARLING, IT'LL BRING BAD LUCK.

I came into the world three years later: Annelies Marie Frank.

GOODNESS, SHE'S EVEN PRETTIER THAN HER SISTER!

YOU'LL BRING BAD LUCK IF YOU SAY THAT!

ACCORDING TO WHOM?

TO US JEWS, OF COURSE!

Being Jewish was not so important in our home. Mother did come from a traditional background, but we kept things religion-free.

But then the Nazis came along and defined us Jews as different after all.

DOES THIS VETERINARIAN ONLY TREAT JEWISH ANIMALS?

NO... BUT HE IS TREATED LIKE AN ANIMAL ONLY BECAUSE HE IS JEWISH...

When the Nazis came to power, their aim was to remove the Jews from German society. Even though Jews were less than 1% of the population, the Nazis believed we were the root of all evil.

ALL MY JEWISH FRIENDS IN THE CIVIL SERVICE HAVE BEEN FIRED. THIS WILL ONLY GET WORSE. IT'S TIME TO MAKE A MOVE.

Believing Holland was safe for Jews, Father moved to Amsterdam in 1933 to run Opekta, a company that manufactured a secret stabilizer for jam.

Mother and Margot followed a bit later, while I stayed in Germany with Grandma.

On Margot's eighth birthday, I came from Germany as a surprise present, and our family was finally reunited.

Life in Holland was beautiful. We had such freedom! We went ice-skating all the time, and even took ski holidays in the Swiss Alps.

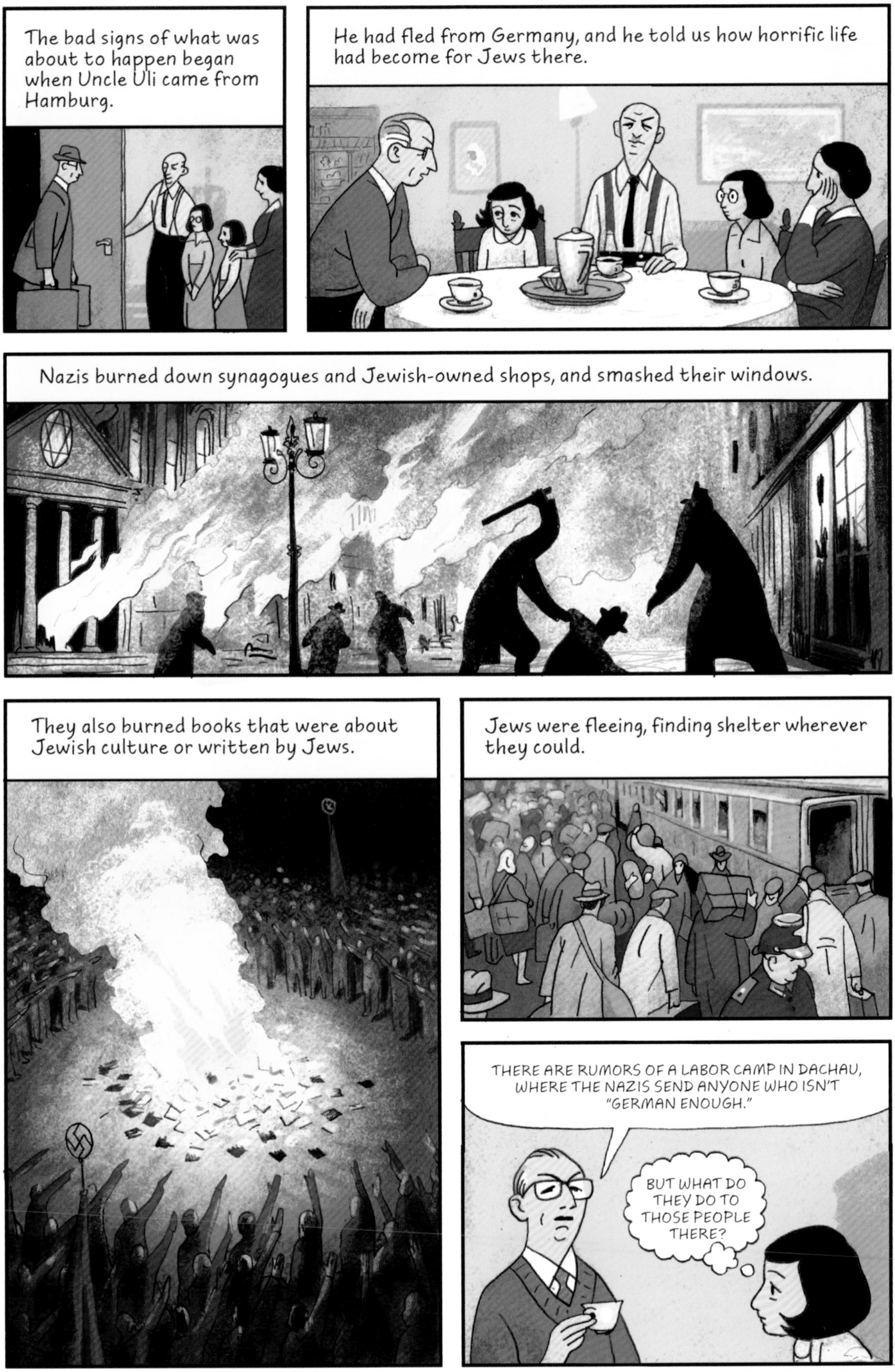

The bad signs of what was about to happen began when Uncle Uli came from Hamburg.
He had fled from Germany, and he told us how horrific life had become for Jews there.
Nazis burned down synagogues and Jewish-owned shops, and smashed their windows.
They also burned books that were about Jewish culture or written by Jews.
Jews were fleeing, finding shelter wherever they could.
THERE ARE RUMORS OF A LABOR CAMP IN DACHAU, WHERE THE NAZIS SEND ANYONE WHO ISN'T "GERMAN ENOUGH."
BUT WHAT DO THEY DO TO THOSE PEOPLE THERE?

Dear Kitty, Who could imagine that after we ran away from the German horrors, the Nazis would invade Holland and it would start all over again...

You see, Kitty, no trams for Jews anymore. Not to mention cars.

AT LEAST WE CAN STILL RIDE OUR BIKES.

Two weeks later... no bikes.

SO NOW WE CAN'T GO TO PARKS, WE CAN'T EVEN BE OUT ON THE STREETS AFTER DARK...

AND WE'RE NOT ALLOWED TO VISIT CHRISTIAN FRIENDS...

AT LEAST THE MOON HAS NO RELIGION...

I NEED TO GO TO THE BATHROOM.

ME TOO, BUT WITH ALL THESE RESTRICTIONS, I DON'T KNOW IF WE'RE ALLOWED TO...

Dearest Kitty,

Recently Mother is always asking me who I'm going to marry when I grow up. But I bet she'll never guess it's my classmate Peter Schiff, because I talked her out of that idea myself, without batting an eyelash.

I love Peter, whom I call Petel, as I've never loved anyone, and I tell myself he's only going around with other girls to hide his feelings for me.

Dearest Kitty, It's sweltering. Everyone is huffing and puffing, and in this heat I have to walk everywhere. Only now do I realize how pleasant a tram is, but we Jews are no longer allowed to make use of this luxury; our own two feet are good enough for us. There are still some good people out there: the ferryman at Jozef Israelskade took us across when we asked him to. It's not the fault of the Dutch that we Jews are having such a bad time.

Dear Kitty, It's only been a few days since we spoke, but a lot has changed.

Something unexpected happened yesterday, when I walked past the bicycle lane.

I'M HELLO, DON'T YOU REMEMBER ME? WILMA'S SECOND COUSIN.

OH, YES...

CAN I ACCOMPANY YOU TO SCHOOL?

It almost looked as if he'd been waiting for me all night.

From that day on, Hello was waiting for me every morning.

It was obvious he was desperately in love with me. And everybody was talking about it...

HE LOOKS OLD ENOUGH TO BE HER UNCLE!

DOESN'T HE HAVE A GIRLFRIEND?

HE IS SO BORING! HOW CAN YOU STAND IT?

TALKING ABOUT BOYS AGAIN, ANNE?

I FIND HIM KIND OF SWEET. VERY POLITE, CLEAN, DECENT LOOKING.

IT DOESN'T MATTER, I'LL NEVER FALL IN LOVE WITH HIM ANYWAY.

WELL, I LIKE HIM. AND AT LEAST I DON'T HAVE TO WORRY ABOUT YOU WANDERING THE DANGEROUS STREETS ALONE, NOW THAT HELLO'S ALWAYS BY YOUR SIDE.

Mr. Kleiman and Mr. Kugler took over Father's company.

Sunday, July 5–Saturday, July 11, 1942

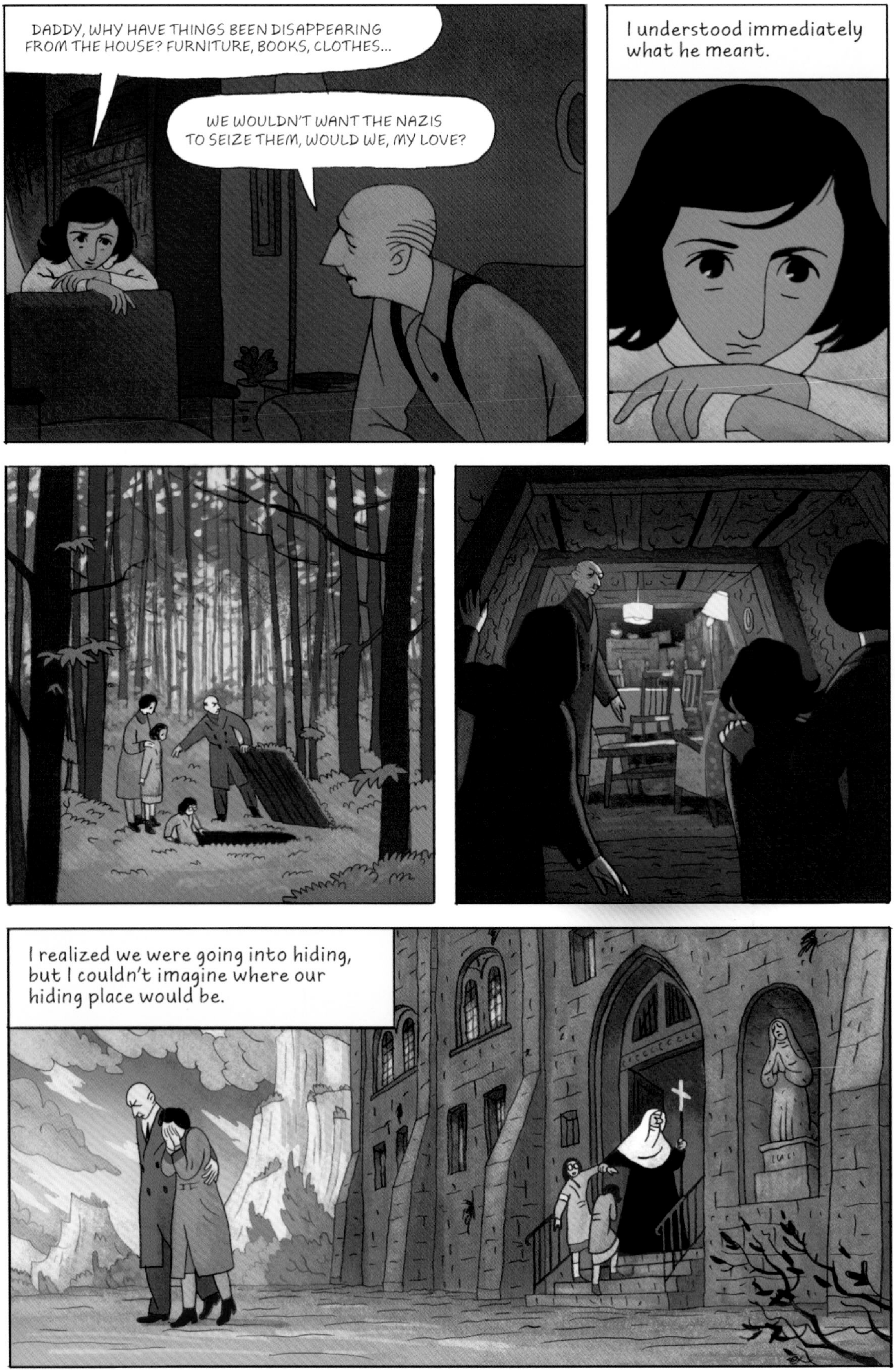
DADDY, WHY HAVE THINGS BEEN DISAPPEARING FROM THE HOUSE? FURNITURE, BOOKS, CLOTHES...
WE WOULDN'T WANT THE NAZIS TO SEIZE THEM, WOULD WE, MY LOVE?
I understood immediately what he meant.
I realized we were going into hiding, but I couldn't imagine where our hiding place would be.

Dearest Kitty, It seems like years since Sunday morning. So much has happened. On Sunday afternoon I came back home from a stroll with Hello, and found Margot and Mother on the couch. Margot was crying and Mother was hugging her. Mother never hugs her.

MARGOT RECEIVED A CALL-UP NOTICE FROM THE SS.

We all knew what a call-up from the Nazi SS meant...

But I also knew Father would never let it happen.

Margot and I immediately started packing our most important belongings into a satchel. Just imagine trying to choose what to take for a life in hiding! It was almost impossible.

I stuck the craziest things in, but I'm not sorry.
Memories mean more to me than dresses.

DON'T YOU THINK YOU SHOULD PACK SOMETHING USEFUL?

USEFUL?! SINCE WHEN HAS BEING USEFUL MADE ANYONE HAPPY IN THIS LIFE?

At midnight, Miep and Jan Gies from Father's company arrived. They took away our belongings to the place where we would be hiding.

DARLING MOORTJE, I CAN'T BELIEVE THIS IS THE LAST TIME WE'LL SNUGGLE TOGETHER.

Mother woke us at 5:30 the next morning. The four of us were wrapped in so many layers of clothes, you would not believe it!

YOU KNOW, ANNE, PERHAPS YOU WERE RIGHT ABOUT THE MEMORIES...

The plan was to make everything look as if we'd run away in a hurry. Father left a note for the neighbor saying we'd fled to Switzerland.

I was terrified. The people we passed were obviously very sorry for us.

There was danger lurking on every street corner.

THOSE JEWS... NEVER WARM ENOUGH FOR THEM...

What a huge surprise it was to arrive at Father's office!

The staff had been informed of our coming, and they welcomed us warmly.

Then I realized how tricky it was to get around Father's office building.
The front is all offices and storerooms...

But no one would suspect that the back contains a whole apartment.

A very steep staircase...Then a cleverly built bookcase that swings out and leads to... the Secret Annex!

OUR ROOM IS SO TINY!

THINK ABOUT THE TRAINS GOING EAST, THEN THE ROOM WILL SEEM HUGE.

SAY GOODBYE TO MOONLIGHT...

After we arrived in the Annex, we learned that Mr. and Mrs. van Daan and their son, Peter, would be hiding with us.

I CAN'T UNDERSTAND WHY FATHER GAVE THE VAN DAANS THE BIGGEST, MOST COMFORTABLE ROOM.

WHY NOT? IT'S JUST LIKE FATHER TO DO THAT!

It took some time before I was able to write to you...

I was worried I might have writer's block, but I am eager to tell you everything...

You no doubt want to hear what I think of being in hiding. Well, all I can say is that I don't really know yet. I don't think I'll ever feel at home in this house, but that doesn't mean I hate it. It's more like being on holiday in some strange hotel.

On our first evening in the Annex, we gathered in the van Daans' room, which is also our shared living room, to listen to the BBC radio broadcast from London.

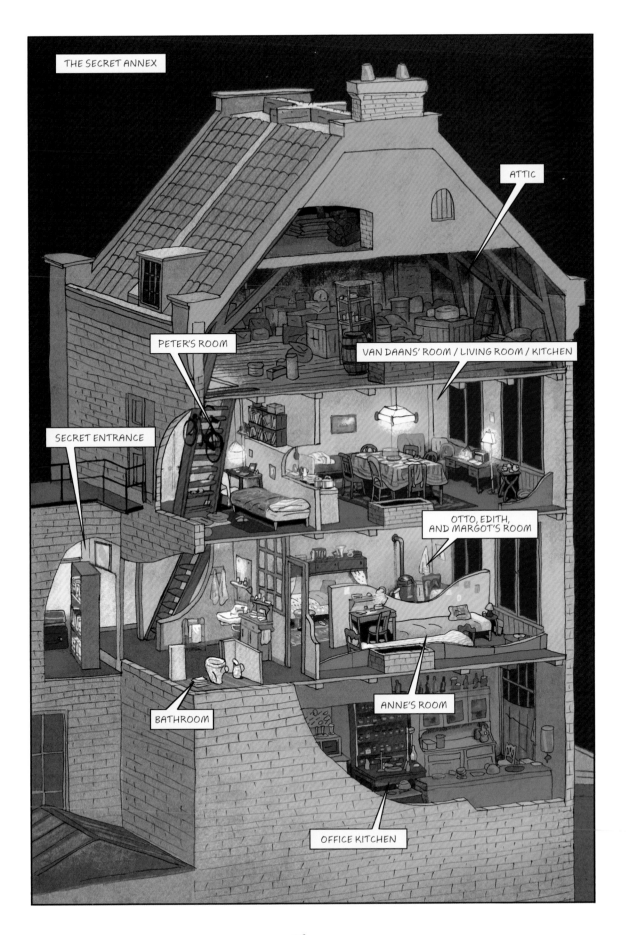

THE SECRET ANNEX

ATTIC

PETER'S ROOM

VAN DAANS' ROOM / LIVING ROOM / KITCHEN

SECRET ENTRANCE

OTTO, EDITH, AND MARGOT'S ROOM

BATHROOM

ANNE'S ROOM

OFFICE KITCHEN

Dear Kitty, Today the van Daans finally joined us in the Annex. As soon as they entered the room, each carrying their most precious possession, I could tell what they would be like. Mr. van Daan is a spice expert who used to work in Father's company. Mrs. van Daan looks like a diva from hell. And their son, Peter, is afraid of his own shadow.

PETER, STOP READING THAT MAGAZINE AND COME DOWN IMMEDIATELY!

IF I MUST DIE HERE, I MIGHT AS WELL BE SITTING ON MY CHAMBER POT.

IF I MUST DIE HERE, I SHALL HAVE ONE MORE CUP OF FINE CHINESE TEA.

I HAVE NO PLANS TO DIE HERE—THERE IS SO MUCH TO LIVE FOR!

I'M SURE EDITH TOO HAS HER OWN PERSONAL HIDING PLACE.

The chamber pot was not the only thing that Madame van Daan kept hidden. Basically, everything considered a "ladies' essential" made a disappearing act.

I HAVE BEEN A LADY ALL MY LIFE, AND I PLAN TO REMAIN A LADY NO MATTER HOW BAD THINGS GET!

YOU WON'T BELIEVE THE RUMORS BEING SPREAD ABOUT YOUR DISAPPEARANCE!

PETER, COME DOWN IMMEDIATELY!

First rumor: "A German SS officer who served with Otto in World War I managed to smuggle you all across the Swiss border."

GOOD AFTERNOON, THE BANK WILL OPEN SOON.
I ASSUME YOU BROUGHT SOME JEWISH MONEY TO DEPOSIT?

Second rumor: "The Franks took off for a long vacation in the countryside."

Third rumor: "A neighbor swears she saw you being loaded into some kind of military vehicle in the middle of the night."

WHY DID YOU HAVE TO MENTION THAT, YOU EVIL MAN!

OH, ANNE, DON'T OVERREACT, HE WAS JUST MAKING A JOKE.

A JOKE? WHAT SORT OF A JOKE IS THAT?!

PETER, COME TO DINNER IMMEDIATELY!!

But Peter never comes down: he's always dying from some horrible disease.

OH, I'M DYING! I HAVE THROAT CANCER!

DEAR GOD! MY LUMBAGO IS KILLING ME!

I'M HAVING A HEART ATTACK! I'M DYING!

HOLY MOSES, MY KIDNEYS ARE FAILING!

So while Peter was dying in his room, obviously it was me who became the center of attention.

EDITH, I WONDER HOW YOU MANAGED TO RAISE TWO COMPLETELY DIFFERENT PERSONALITIES—ANNE AND MARGOT—IN THE SAME HOUSE...

MIND YOU, LADIES, I'M IN THE ROOM.

I WONDER WHY YOU DIDN'T WEAR YOUR FUR COAT TODAY. IT'S PRETTY CHILLY OUTSIDE, ISN'T IT?

IF ONLY YOU WOULD LEARN SOME MANNERS FROM YOUR SISTER!

It's always about me and my sister...

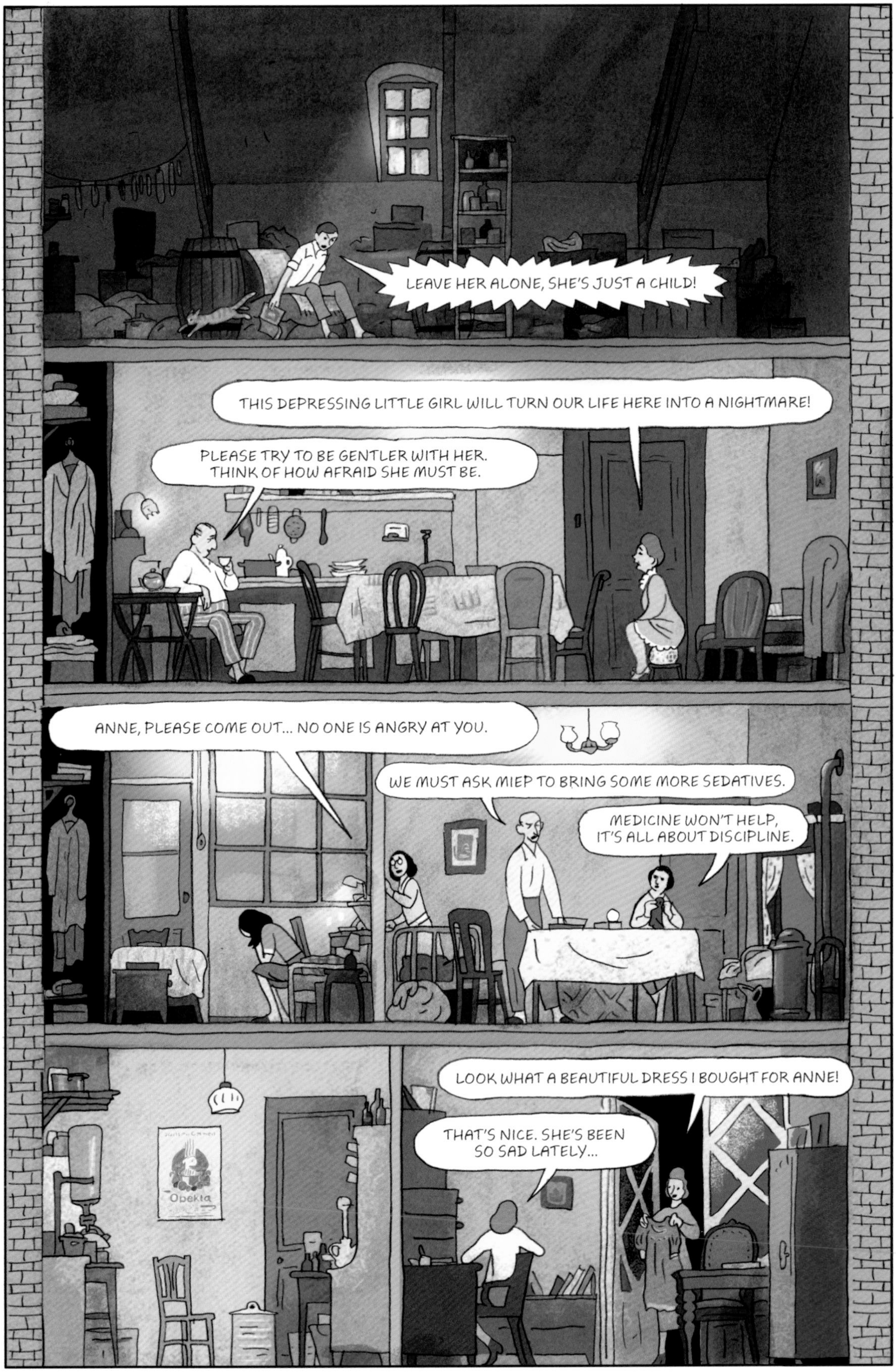
LEAVE HER ALONE, SHE'S JUST A CHILD!
THIS DEPRESSING LITTLE GIRL WILL TURN OUR LIFE HERE INTO A NIGHTMARE!
PLEASE TRY TO BE GENTLER WITH HER. THINK OF HOW AFRAID SHE MUST BE.
ANNE, PLEASE COME OUT... NO ONE IS ANGRY AT YOU.
WE MUST ASK MIEP TO BRING SOME MORE SEDATIVES.
MEDICINE WON'T HELP, IT'S ALL ABOUT DISCIPLINE.
LOOK WHAT A BEAUTIFUL DRESS I BOUGHT FOR ANNE!
THAT'S NICE. SHE'S BEEN SO SAD LATELY...

Dear Kitty, Since the van Daans' arrival, we have had a regular daily routine. In the mornings, while the workers are busy downstairs, we must remain deadly quiet. That is when we study and learn things by heart.

At 12:30 p.m. the warehouse men go home for lunch and the whole gang breathes a sigh of relief. Bep and Miep from the office bring us food, but we must eat in complete silence.

I mean, those who can be silent for three minutes straight.

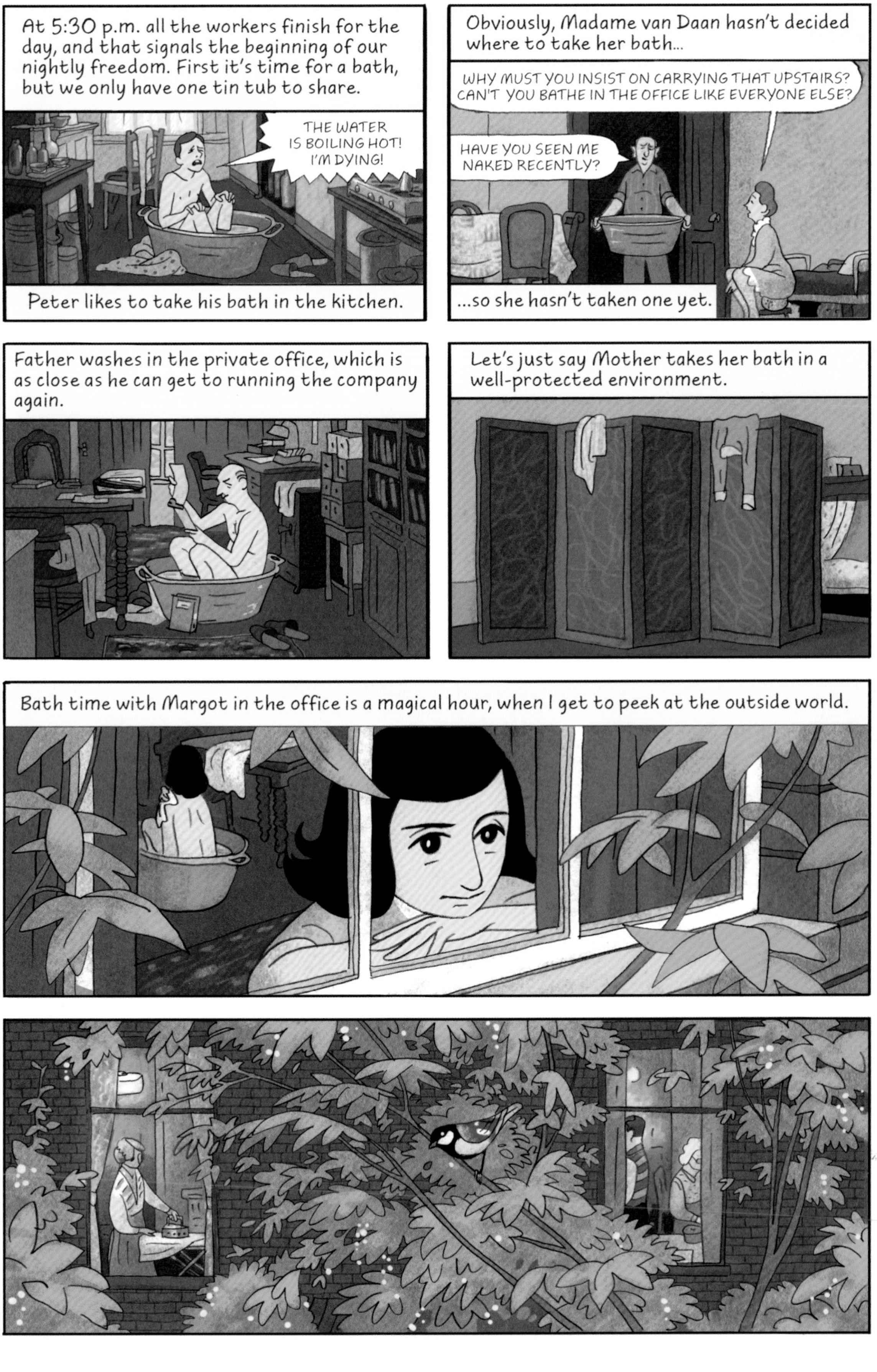
At 5:30 p.m. all the workers finish for the day, and that signals the beginning of our nightly freedom. First it's time for a bath, but we only have one tin tub to share.
THE WATER IS BOILING HOT! I'M DYING!
Peter likes to take his bath in the kitchen.
Obviously, Madame van Daan hasn't decided where to take her bath...
WHY MUST YOU INSIST ON CARRYING THAT UPSTAIRS? CAN'T YOU BATHE IN THE OFFICE LIKE EVERYONE ELSE?
HAVE YOU SEEN ME NAKED RECENTLY?
...so she hasn't taken one yet.
Father washes in the private office, which is as close as he can get to running the company again.
Let's just say Mother takes her bath in a well-protected environment.
Bath time with Margot in the office is a magical hour, when I get to peek at the outside world.

It's time for dinner.

PRINCESS JULIANA IS EXPECTING A BABY IN JANUARY.

OH... THIS IS SO BORING!

BORING? IT'S THE MOST EXCITING NEWS I'VE HEARD SINCE WE CAME HERE!

At night, the bad thoughts creep into my mind...

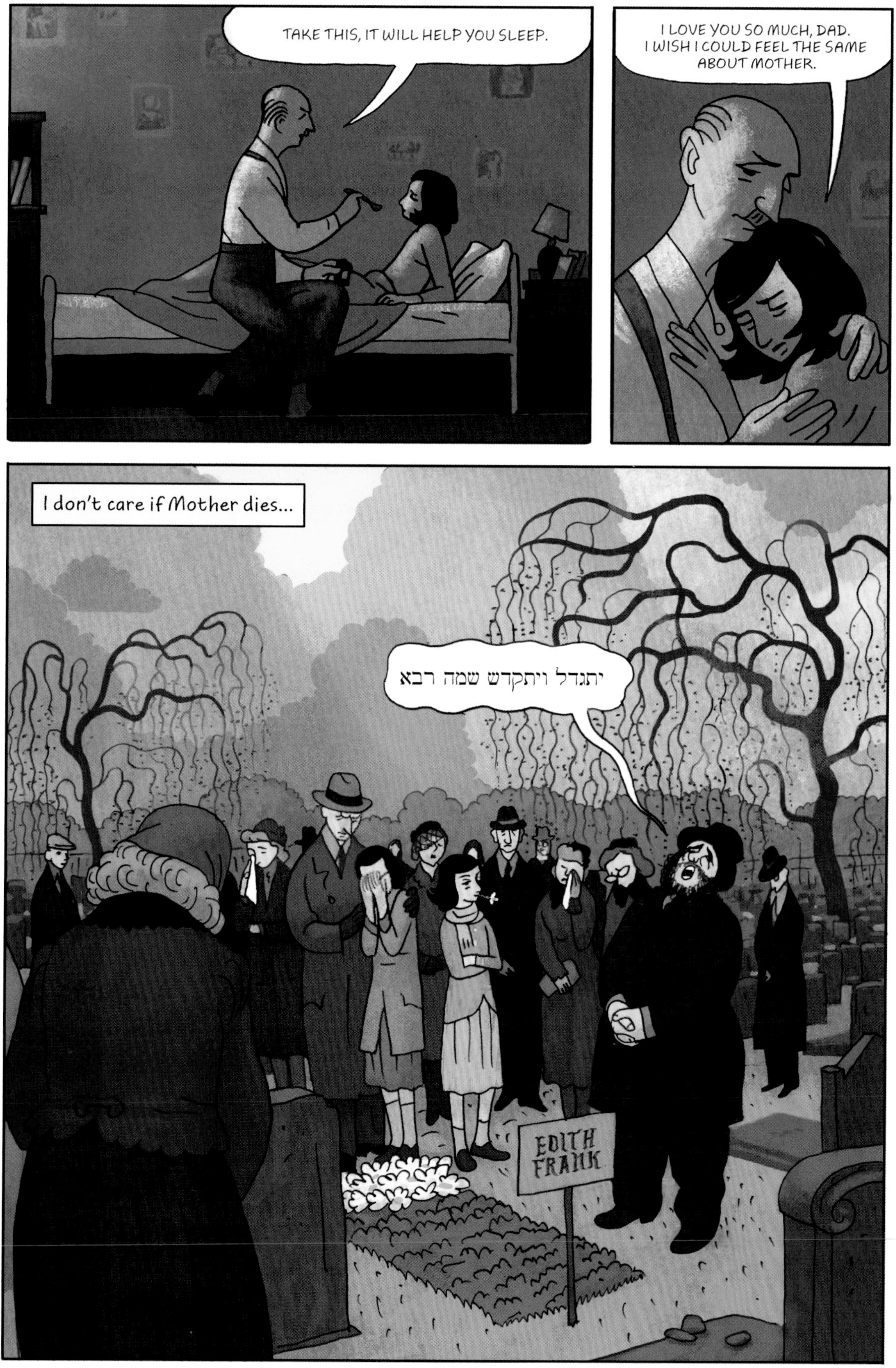
TAKE THIS, IT WILL HELP YOU SLEEP.
I LOVE YOU SO MUCH, DAD. I WISH I COULD FEEL THE SAME ABOUT MOTHER.
I don't care if Mother dies...
יתגדל ויתקדש שמה רבא
EDITH FRANK

Dearest Kitty,

I'm dying to tell you about another one of our clashes, but before I do I'd like to say this: I think it's odd that grown-ups quarrel so easily and so often and about such petty matters. Up till now I always thought bickering was just something children did and that they outgrew it. Of course, there's sometimes a reason to have a "real" quarrel, but the verbal exchanges that take place here are just plain bickering. They refer to these as "discussions" instead of "quarrels," but Germans don't know the difference! They criticize everything, and I mean everything, about me: my behavior, my personality, my manners; every inch of me, from head to toe and back again, is the subject of gossip and debate. Harsh words and shouts are constantly being flung at my head, though I'm absolutely not used to it. According to the powers that be, I'm supposed to grin and bear it. But I can't! I have no intention of taking their insults lying down. I'll show them that Anne Frank wasn't born yesterday. They'll sit up and take notice and keep their big mouths shut when I make them see they ought to attend to their own manners instead of mine. How dare they behave like that! It's simply barbaric.

But enough of that. I've bored you long enough with my quarrels, and yet I can't resist adding a highly interesting dinner conversation.

Somehow we landed on the subject of Pim's extreme diffidence. His modesty is a well-known fact, which even the stupidest person wouldn't dream of questioning. All of a sudden Mrs. van Daan, who feels the need to bring herself into every conversation, remarked, "I'm very modest and retiring too, much more so than my husband!"

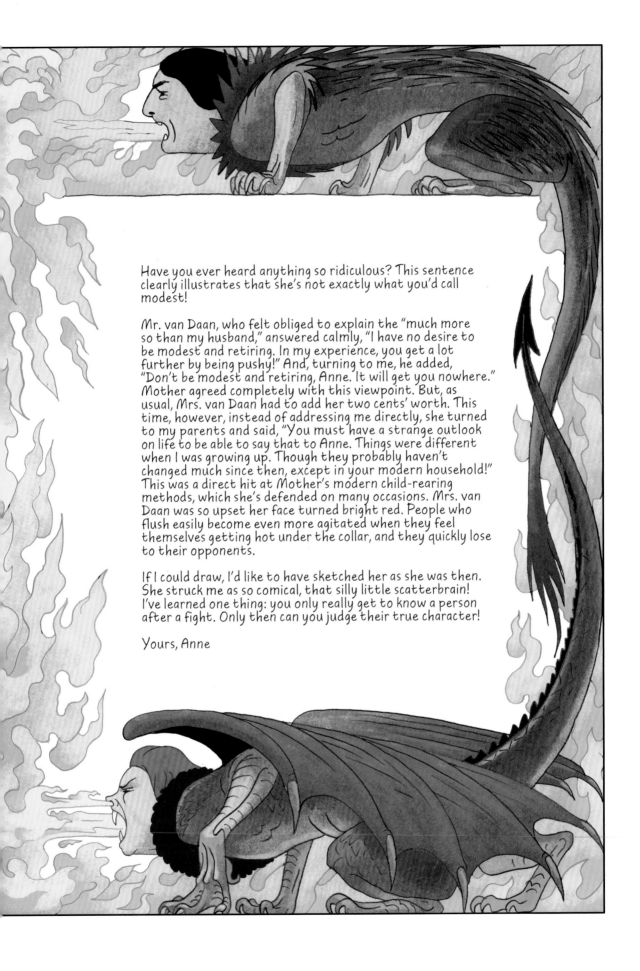

Have you ever heard anything so ridiculous? This sentence clearly illustrates that she's not exactly what you'd call modest!

Mr. van Daan, who felt obliged to explain the "much more so than my husband," answered calmly, "I have no desire to be modest and retiring. In my experience, you get a lot further by being pushy!" And, turning to me, he added, "Don't be modest and retiring, Anne. It will get you nowhere." Mother agreed completely with this viewpoint. But, as usual, Mrs. van Daan had to add her two cents' worth. This time, however, instead of addressing me directly, she turned to my parents and said, "You must have a strange outlook on life to be able to say that to Anne. Things were different when I was growing up. Though they probably haven't changed much since then, except in your modern household!" This was a direct hit at Mother's modern child-rearing methods, which she's defended on many occasions. Mrs. van Daan was so upset her face turned bright red. People who flush easily become even more agitated when they feel themselves getting hot under the collar, and they quickly lose to their opponents.

If I could draw, I'd like to have sketched her as she was then. She struck me as so comical, that silly little scatterbrain! I've learned one thing: you only really get to know a person after a fight. Only then can you judge their true character!

Yours, Anne

Saturday, October 3-Wednesday, October 7, 1942

Dearest Kitty, Ive been allowed to read more grown-up books lately. <u>Eva's Youth</u> by Nico van Suchtelen is currently keeping me busy.

Eva thought that children grew on trees, like apples.

She thought cats laid eggs and hatched them like chickens...
Eva wanted a baby too.

She took a woolen scarf and spread it on the ground so the egg could fall into it. She squatted down and began to push. She clucked as she waited, but no egg came out... only something smelly that looked like a sausage. Eventually Eva grew up and realized women don't lay eggs.

Some women have to sell their bodies on the street to make money.

I imagine that... I've gone to Switzerland. Daddy and I sleep in one room, in my father's family's huge mansion in the Alps.

That sort of daydream, with so many details, is what happens when you're in hiding for an unknown period of time.

Today Miep told us some terrible news from the real world: she saw her Jewish neighbor taken away by the Gestapo, and she could do nothing to help her.

Later, she met someone who'd managed to escape from a concentration camp. When Miep asked about her neighbor, the man said she'd probably been transported to Westerbork in a cattle car.

It must be terrible in Westerbork. The people get almost nothing to eat, much less to drink, as water is available only one hour a day, and there's only one lavatory and sink for several thousand people... We assume that most of the people in the faraway camps are being murdered. The English radio says they're being gassed. Perhaps that's the quickest way to die.

39

Dear Kitty, Yesterday was Peter's birthday.
At 8 a.m. sharp I was already in his attic.

SO, WHAT PRESENTS DID YOU GET?

I DIDN'T KNOW YOU SMOKED...

SOMETIMES I DO. IT MAKES ME LOOK DISTINGUISHED...

In honor of Peter's birthday, we had news that the English had landed in Tunis, Algiers, and Casablanca!

AS CHURCHILL SAYS, "THIS IS NOT THE BEGINNING OF THE END. BUT IT IS, PERHAPS, THE END OF THE BEGINNING."

Yet another reason for optimism on Peter's birthday: the Russian city of Stalingrad still hasn't fallen into German hands.

In the true spirit of the Annex, I should talk to you about food.

Every day Mr. Kleiman meets his secret baker and buys two loaves.
But the price goes up each time.

Of course, we don't have as much as we did at home, but it is enough.

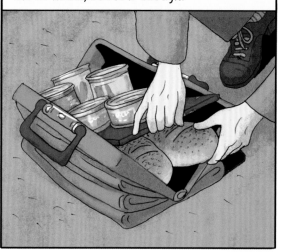

We have about a hundred cans of food stored in the Annex, but mostly our supplies include cabbage, meatloaf, and pickles.

And then there's the beans... We must have 300 pounds of them, all stored in sacks.

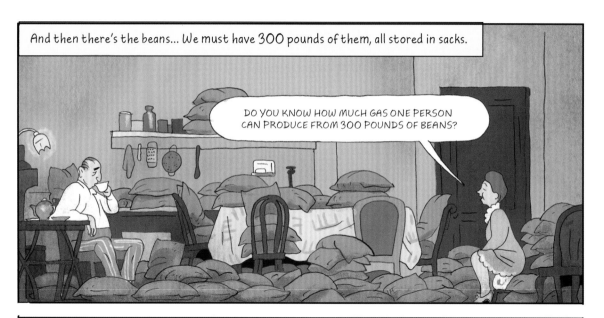

DO YOU KNOW HOW MUCH GAS ONE PERSON CAN PRODUCE FROM 300 POUNDS OF BEANS?

The beans were hanging all over our living space, so we decided to move them to the attic.

But one sack broke, and a flood, or rather a hailstorm, of brown beans went flying through the air and down the stairs. It made enough noise to raise the dead. At first we thought we were being bombed.

We had to pick up every single bean: you never know how desperate you might become for one tasty bean in the future.

Dear Kitty, Yesterday Father gave me some great news!

MY DARLING, WE ARE PLANNING TO RESCUE ANOTHER JEW, WHO WILL STAY WITH US IN THE ANNEX. HE WILL HAVE TO SLEEP IN YOUR ROOM, ANNE.

OF COURSE, DADDY. I'LL DO WHATEVER IT TAKES TO SAVE ONE MORE LIFE.

But after Father left, I realized I would have to say farewell to the privilege of being alone with you, Kitty, whenever I want to.

My new roommate is named Albert Dussel. He is Miep's dentist.

I DON'T KNOW WHAT TO DO... I MUST FIND A PLACE TO HIDE!

I MIGHT HAVE A SOLUTION FOR YOU. JUST DON'T PULL OUT ALL MY TEETH!

Three days later, Mr. Dussel arrived at the Annex. He brought all his dental tools.

OTTO FRANK?! I DON'T BELIEVE IT! I THOUGHT YOU'D ESCAPED WITH YOUR FAMILY TO SWITZERLAND.

IN THAT CASE, OUR TRICK WORKED!

Later on Margot and I took a peek at his tools.

OH DEAR, THAT IS SICK. AND FRIGHTENING...

LET'S HOPE HE HAS SOME LAUGHING GAS, TOO...

I had prepared a brochure for Mr. Dussel, to explain the regulations at the Annex.

Price: Free!!!

The Secret Annex

A Unique Facility for the Temporary Accommodation of Jews and Other Dispossessed Persons

Location: Beautiful, quiet, wooded surroundings in the heart of Amsterdam. No private residences in vicinity.

Food: Low-fat only! Breakfast: 9:00 a.m. (in silence, excluding weekends). Lunch 1:15–1:45 (in silence, excluding weekends). Dinner: Depends on news broadcasts.

During mealtimes: No German stations allowed.

Alcohol: For medicinal purposes only.

Pets: Only in the attic.

Baths: At your own risk, at nighttime or on weekends.

Mr. Dussel has told us much about the outside world we've missed for so long.

HOW MUCH FOR A FAMILY OF FIVE JEWS?

FIFTEEN GUILDERS PER HEAD.

GO TO NO. 15, THIRD FLOOR, LEFT DOOR. FIVE HEADS.

It's like the slave hunt of the olden days.

In the evenings, when it's dark, I often see long lines of good, innocent people, accompanied by crying children, walking on and on until they nearly drop. No one is spared. The sick, the elderly, children, babies—all are marched to their death.

Friday, November 20, 1942

Dearest Kitty,

We don't really know how to react. Up till now very little news about the Jews had reached us here, and we thought it best to stay as cheerful as possible. Every now and then Miep used to mention what had happened to a friend, and Mother or Mrs. van Daan would start to cry, so she decided it was better not to say any more. But we bombarded Mr. Dussel with questions, and the stories he had to tell were so gruesome and dreadful that we can't get them out of our heads.

Once we've had time to digest the news, we'll probably go back to our usual joking and teasing. It won't do us or those outside any good if we continue to be as gloomy as we are now. And what would be the point of turning the Secret Annex into a Melancholy Annex?

No matter what I'm doing, I can't help thinking about those who are gone. I catch myself laughing and remember that it's a disgrace to be so cheerful. But am I supposed to spend the whole day crying? No, I can't do that. This gloom will pass.

Added to this misery there's another, but of a more personal nature, and it pales in comparison to the suffering I've just told you about. Still, I can't help telling you that lately I've begun to feel deserted. I'm surrounded by too great a void. I never used to give it much thought, since my mind was filled with my friends and having a good time. Now I think either about unhappy things or about myself. It's taken a while, but I've finally realized that Father, no matter how kind he may be, can't take the place of my former world. When it comes to my feelings, Mother and Margot ceased to count long ago.

But why do I bother you with this foolishness? I'm terribly ungrateful, Kitty, I know, but when I've been scolded for the umpteenth time and have all these other woes to think about as well, my head begins to reel!

Yours, Anne

Dear Kitty, At last, after six months in the Annex, I've discovered the one thing Mr. van Daan is good at. It happened one day when Mr. Kleiman arrived with a grin on his face.

LOOK WHAT A DEAL I GOT ON THE BLACK MARKET!

ISN'T HE PAST HIS EXPIRATION DATE...?

IT'S A SHE, DADDY.

FINALLY, AFTER SIX MONTHS! THIS IS A DREAM COME TRUE.

Mr. van Daan was hired for his knowledge of spices, and yet, to our great delight, it's his sausage talents that have come in handy.
(He likes to eat them, too...)

USING MY SECRET SPICE BLEND, WE'LL HAVE ENOUGH TO LIVE ON FOR LONGER THAN THE HUNDRED YEARS' WAR BETWEEN ENGLAND AND FRANCE!

I CAN'T KEEP STIRRING THIS SOUP—MY BACK ACHES!

WELL, MAYBE YOU SHOULDN'T HAVE GROWN SUCH A FAT BEHIND SINCE ARRIVING HERE...

DIDN'T NAPOLEON DIE FROM EATING TOO MUCH PRESERVED MEAT?

HE DID, BUT THAT'S BECAUSE THE POOR MAN DIDN'T HAVE MY SECRET FORMULA.

It was obvious that poor Hermann van Daan was grabbing far too much attention. So much so that the two ladies of the Annex had to react.

After a great deal of squirming, kicking, and screaming, the job was done. I must say, the patient showed the utmost bravery.

Madame was soon back at work in the kitchen, but one thing is certain: it'll be a while before she makes another dental appointment!

Yesterday afternoon, while Margot and I were bathing in the office, I peered out through a chink in the heavy curtains.

DON'T GET TOO CLOSE TO THE WINDOW...

The children in our neighborhood are so dirty you wouldn't want to touch them with a barge pole.

What if I took a fishing rod and reeled in each of those kids, stuck them in the tub, washed and mended their clothes...

AND THEN TOMORROW THEY'D BE JUST AS DIRTY AND TATTERED AS THEY WERE BEFORE.

Then it started raining hard, and all I could see was a sea of umbrellas. But by now I can recognize the women at a glance: gone to fat from eating potatoes, dressed in a red or green coat and worn-out shoes...

Then something extraordinary happened: I recognized two Jews I knew from our old neighborhood.

I felt as though I were gazing at one of the Seven Wonders of the World.

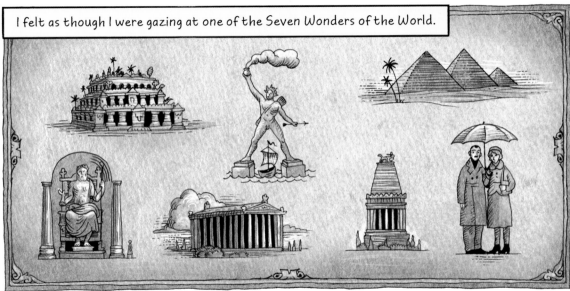

WHICH WONDER WOULD YOU GIVE UP TO SAVE THE JEWS?

PROBABLY THE LIGHTHOUSE. WE WON'T BE RESCUED BY A BOAT ANYWAY...

It gave me such a funny feeling, as if I'd denounced them to the authorities and was now spying on their misfortune.

Tuesday, December 22, 1942

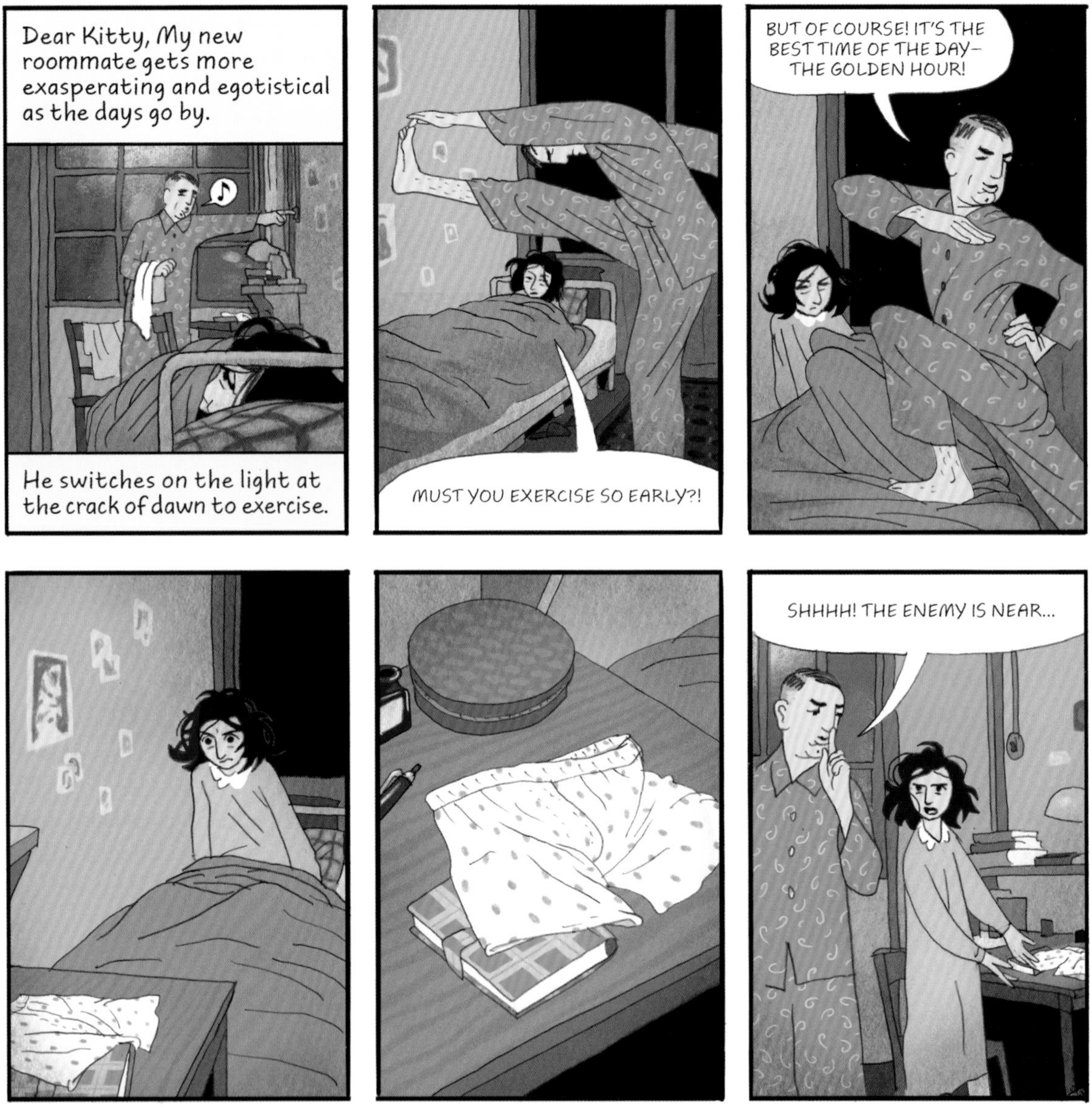
Dear Kitty, My new roommate gets more exasperating and egotistical as the days go by.
He switches on the light at the crack of dawn to exercise.
MUST YOU EXERCISE SO EARLY?!
BUT OF COURSE! IT'S THE BEST TIME OF THE DAY— THE GOLDEN HOUR!
SHHHH! THE ENEMY IS NEAR...

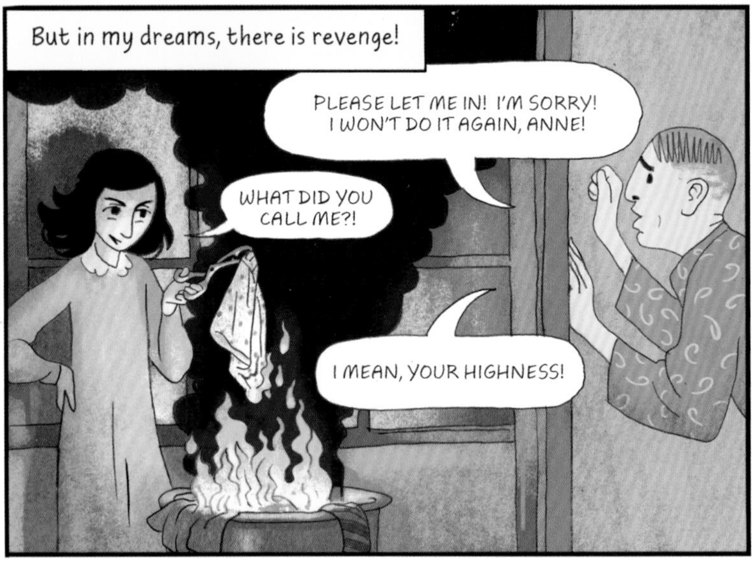
But in my dreams, there is revenge!
PLEASE LET ME IN! I'M SORRY! I WON'T DO IT AGAIN, ANNE!
WHAT DID YOU CALL ME?!
I MEAN, YOUR HIGHNESS!

Oh, I'm becoming so sensible! We've got to be reasonable about everything we do here. Studying, listening, holding our tongues, helping others, being kind, making compromises, and I don't know what else! I'm afraid my common sense, which was in short supply to begin with, will be used up too quickly and I won't have any left by the time the war is over.

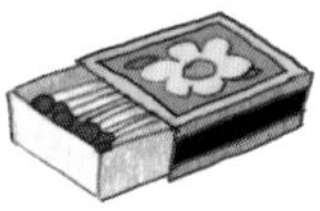

Saturday, January 30, 1943

Dearest Kitty,

I'm seething with rage, yet I can't show it. I'd like to scream, stamp my foot, give Mother a good shaking, cry, and I don't know what else because of the nasty words, mocking looks, and accusations that she hurls at me day after day, piercing me like arrows from a tightly strung bow, which are nearly impossible to pull from my body. I'd like to scream at Mother, Margot, the van Daans, Dussel, and Father too: "Leave me alone, let me have at least one night when I don't cry myself to sleep with my eyes burning and my head pounding. Let me get away, away from everything, away from this world!"

But I can't do that. I can't let them see my doubts, or the wounds they've inflicted on me. I couldn't bear their sympathy or their good-humored derision. It would only make me want to scream even more.

Everyone thinks I'm showing off when I talk, ridiculous when I'm silent, insolent when I answer, cunning when I have a good idea, lazy when I'm tired, selfish when I eat one bite more than I should, stupid, cowardly, calculating, etc., etc. All day long I hear nothing but what an exasperating child I am, and although I laugh it off and pretend not to mind, I do mind. I wish I could ask God to give me another personality, one that doesn't antagonize everyone.

But that's impossible. I'm stuck with the character I was born with, and yet I'm sure I'm not a bad person. I do my best to please everyone, more than they'd ever suspect in a million years. When I'm upstairs, I try to laugh it off, because I don't want them to see my troubles.

It's impossible for me to be all smiles one day and venomous the next. I'd rather choose the golden mean, which isn't so golden, and keep my thoughts to myself. Perhaps sometime I'll treat the others with the same contempt as they treat me.

Oh, if only I could.

Yours, Anne

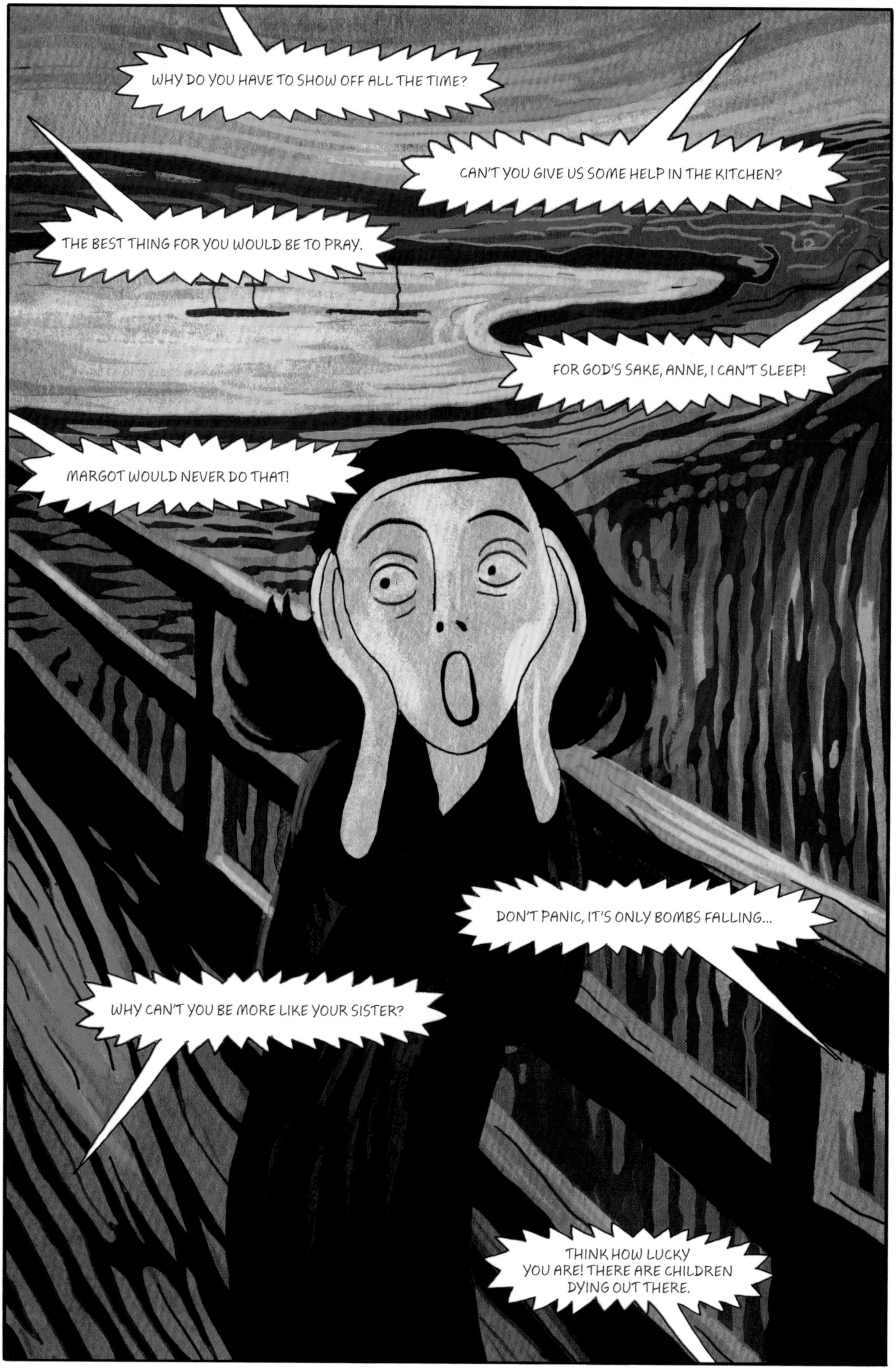
WHY DO YOU HAVE TO SHOW OFF ALL THE TIME?
CAN'T YOU GIVE US SOME HELP IN THE KITCHEN?
THE BEST THING FOR YOU WOULD BE TO PRAY.
FOR GOD'S SAKE, ANNE, I CAN'T SLEEP!
MARGOT WOULD NEVER DO THAT!
DON'T PANIC, IT'S ONLY BOMBS FALLING...
WHY CAN'T YOU BE MORE LIKE YOUR SISTER?
THINK HOW LUCKY YOU ARE! THERE ARE CHILDREN DYING OUT THERE.

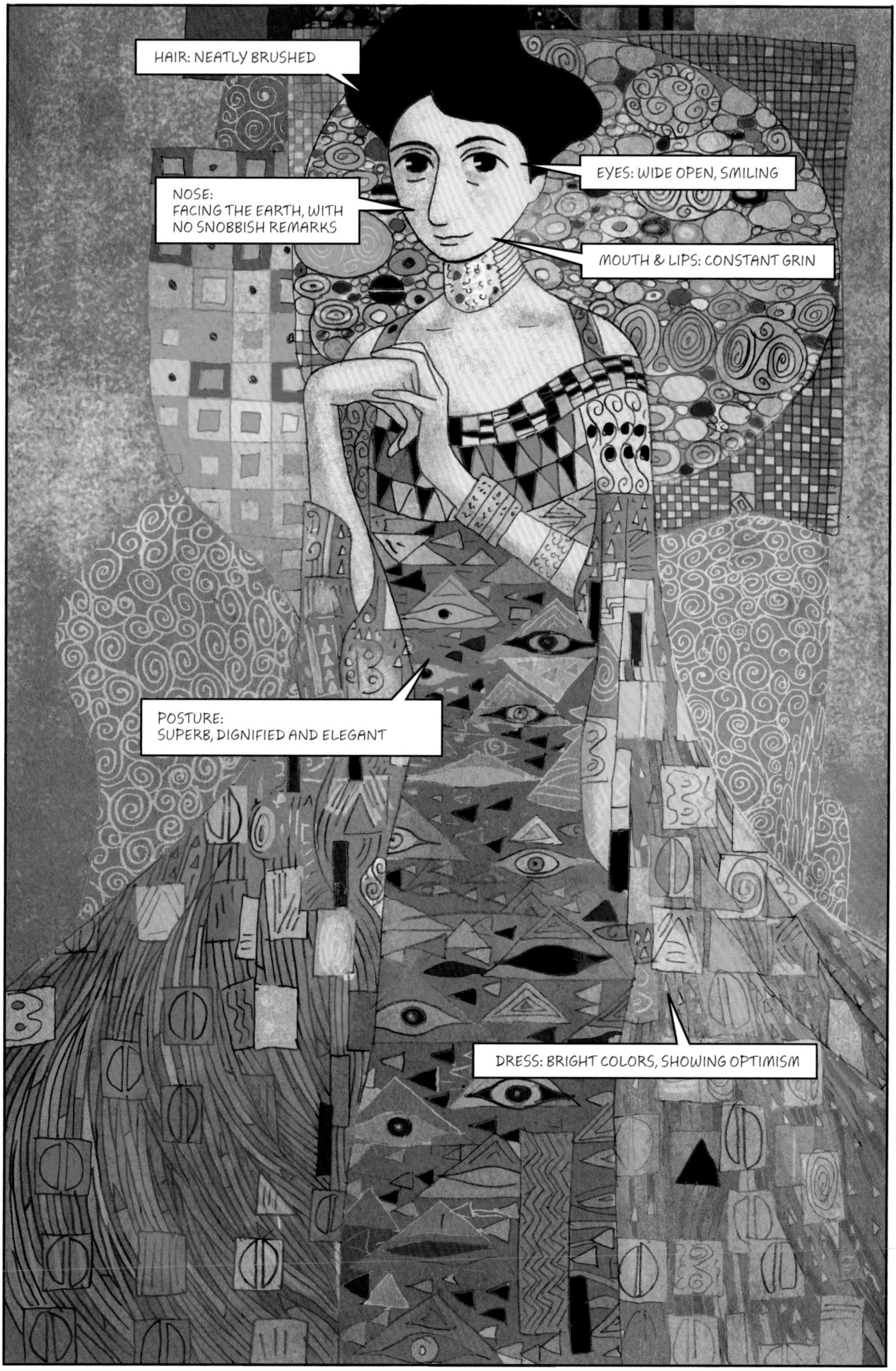
HAIR: NEATLY BRUSHED
EYES: WIDE OPEN, SMILING
NOSE:
FACING THE EARTH, WITH
NO SNOBBISH REMARKS
MOUTH & LIPS: CONSTANT GRIN
POSTURE:
SUPERB, DIGNIFIED AND ELEGANT
DRESS: BRIGHT COLORS, SHOWING OPTIMISM

Wednesday, March 10, 1943

Dearest Kitty, We had a short circuit last night, and besides that, the guns were booming away until dawn. I still haven't got over my fear of planes and shooting, and I crawl into Father's bed nearly every night for comfort.

I'M SORRY, I'M SO CHILDISH.

DON'T BE SORRY, EVERYONE IN THE ANNEX HAS THEIR FEARS.

Madame's biggest fear is burglars.

HERMANN!! WAKE UP! I HEAR FOOTSTEPS DOWNSTAIRS!

IT'S ONLY YOUR HEART BEATING...

And Peter's biggest fear is rats.

IT BIT MY HAND OFF!

The other Annex dwellers all share one fear:

I'M TELLING YOU, ANNE WILL GET US ALL CAPTURED.

I AGREE. HER BEHAVIOR IS OUT OF CONTROL!

OH, STOP BEING SO HARD ON HER.

Friday, March 19, 1943

 Mr. Dussel is terribly sad, because he misses his beloved Lotje so much.

MY DEAREST ALBERT, I FEEL SO GUILTY ABOUT BEING CHRISTIAN, LIVING IN SAFETY AS IF NOTHING WERE HAPPENING.

 START WRITING, MARGOT: "MY DEAR LOTJE, IF LONGING FOR SOMEONE CAN KILL, I AM A DEAD MAN NOW."

 He made Miep and Bep play Cupid by delivering his letters to Lotje.

 But when Father found out...

ALBERT, DON'T YOU EVER DARE SEND YOUR LETTERS AGAIN! IF ANYONE FOUND OUT, ALL EIGHT OF US WOULD BE DEAD!

 MARGOT, I'M SURPRISED AT YOU. I WOULD NOT HAVE EXPECTED THIS.

OH, BUT IT WAS ALL FOR LOVE!

 Well, at least being executed for the sake of love would be a good way to go.

Dear Kitty, At this critical time for Father's company, three of our four saviors are out of commission.

Mr. Kleiman had to have more surgery on his intestines.

Bep has a terrible case of the flu.

And Mr. Voskuijl has an ulcer attack.

Since everyone was ill, Mr. Kugler had a big day: he had to meet with a German delegation for a very important business transaction.

YOU KNOW I HAVE COMPLETE TRUST IN YOU.

DON'T MAKE ME MORE NERVOUS THAN I ALREADY AM!

PRETEND THE LEADING ACTOR IS SICK, AND THIS IS YOUR BIG BREAK!

TO BE OR NOT TO BE, THAT IS THE QUESTION...

WE'LL HAVE TO TAKE SHIFTS EAVESDROPPING ON THE MEETING. HERE, LIKE THIS...

YOU MUST REMEMBER EVERY WORD BY HEART.

CAN'T WE JUST WRITE DOWN WHAT THEY'RE SAYING?

NO! THEY'LL HEAR THE PEN SCRATCHING THE PAPER.

First Mother and Father took their posts.

Then it was Margot's and my turn.

The minute our shift began, I fell into a deep sleep...

Tuesday, April 27, 1943

Dear Kitty, British air strikes are increasing daily. The Carlton Hotel has been destroyed. British planes landed firebombs right on top of the German Officers' Club.
We haven't had a good night's rest in ages.

At these times of curfew and no supplies from our guardian angels, our food has become a biological experiment.

THE COFFEE IS FAKE ANYWAY. NO POINT IN WAKING UP.

I DON'T RECALL FROM MY SCHOOL DAYS THAT VEGETABLES CAN TURN INTO ANIMALS.

COME ON, MOUSCHI, YOU BEAST, LET'S SEE YOU EAT THIS.

I WONDER IF THAT'S WHAT THEY GIVE THEM TO EAT IN THE CAMPS.

I'D RATHER EAT MY TOBACCO AND DIE OF DIARRHEA.

I'D RATHER EAT MY LIVER AND DIE RIGHT AWAY.

One thing goes without saying: if you're trying to slim down, the Annex is the place to be!

But not everyone is on the low-fat diet. Mr. Dussel sits alone in the dark, delighting in the goodies his beloved Lotje sends him.

Dear Kitty, Just as we thought we were entering silent and peaceful times at last, the guns started banging away like crazy. So much so that I had to pack and unpack my "escape bag" four times, in case we have to flee on short notice.

WHAT ARE YOU DOING?

RUNNING AWAY, OF COURSE!

RUNNING AWAY? WHERE WOULD YOU GO? COME AND COMB MY HAIR INSTEAD.

YOUR HAIR IS LIKE TAR...

IT'S NOT MY HAIR, IT'S THE COMB.

It was true: the comb had only eight teeth left.

The state of the comb inspired me to examine the state of things after a year in the Annex.

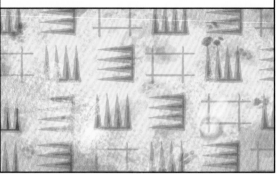

The oilcloth on the dining table, for example, has never been washed!

Father's tie: moth-eaten!

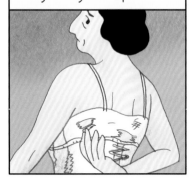

Mother's corset: frayed beyond repair!

Margot's bra: at least two sizes too small!

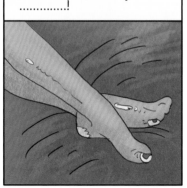

Madame's stockings: ....!

The van Daans' linens: haven't been washed all year!

I sometimes wonder: How can we, whose every possession, from my panties to Father's shaving brush, is so old and worn, ever hope to regain the position we had before the war?

Dearest Kitty, Who would have thought I would still be here, a year after moving into the Annex, celebrating another birthday? It can't compare to last year's celebration, but Father composed a poem for me that is too nice to keep to myself:

As youngest among us, but small no more,
Your life can be trying, for we have the chore
Of becoming your teachers, a terrible bore.
"We've got experience! Take it from me!"
"We've done this all before, you see.
We know the ropes, we know the game."
Since time immemorial, always the same.
One's own shortcomings are nothing but fluff,
But everyone else's are heavier stuff.
Fault-finding comes easy when this is our plight,
But it's hard for your parents, try as they might,
To treat you with fairness, and kindness as well;
Nit-picking's a habit that's hard to dispel.
When you're living with old folk, all you can do
Is put up with their nagging—it's hard but it's true.
The pill may be bitter, but down it must go,
For it's meant to keep the peace, you know.
The many months here have not been in vain,
Since wasting time goes against your grain.
You read and study nearly all the day,
Determined to chase the boredom away.
The more difficult question, much harder to bear,
Is "What on earth do I have to wear?
I've got no more panties, my clothes are too tight,
My shirt is a loincloth, I'm really a sight!
To put on my shoes I must cut off my toes,
Oh dear, I'm plagued with so many woes!"

As if my birthday weren't depressing enough, we just learned that we are about to lose two of our greatest supporters. First, Mr. Voskuijl: He went in for surgery on his ulcer, but they discovered he has very advanced cancer. He doesn't have much time left. Now the good man can no longer let us know what's being said and done in the warehouse. He was a great source of help and support.

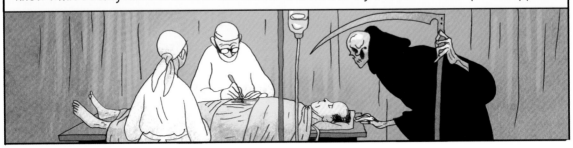

And second, our trusty old radio will soon be gone!

We must turn it in to the Nazi authorities, who don't want any civilians to hear news from the front.

Sunday, July 11, 1943

Dear Kitty, I can see that a little hypocrisy gets me a lot further than my old method of saying exactly what I think.

OH, HOW GORGEOUS YOU LOOK! JUST LIKE A PARISIAN MODEL!

WILL YOU PRAY WITH ME?

OF COURSE, MOMMY, ALTHOUGH I ALREADY PRAYED THIS MORNING.

DEAR LORD: PLEASE GRANT ME THE POWER TO REMAIN HYPOCRITICAL FOREVER AND EVER...

I LOVE YOUR NEW TIE CLIP.

THAT'S NOT A CLIP, IT'S JUST A STAIN.

That's when I realized I've become very nearsighted.

DEAREST, I THINK IT WOULD BE BEST FOR BEP TO TAKE YOU TO AN EYE DOCTOR.

ABSOLUTELY NOT! IT'S TOO DANGEROUS!

WE'LL DRESS HER UP, NO ONE WILL SUSPECT SHE'S JEWISH.

FIRST PUT ON THIS RAINCOAT.

THEN THESE SUNGLASSES. WHO WOULD RECOGNIZE YOU AS A JEW?

NOW TRY ON THIS HAT.

The thought of going outside—walking down the street!—was petrifying. I think I'd rather go blind and die of starvation in the Annex.

There's been a break-in—a real one!

Peter went down to the warehouse this morning and realized there were burglars there. He immediately reported to Daddy and we all stayed upstairs the whole day. In such cases our orders are "not to wash ourselves or run any water, to be quiet, and not to go to the lavatory." Finally, we got the all-clear from Mr. Kleiman, but in the meantime we all froze our human existence. Very scary. I'm sure we all lost kilos during those long hours.

The burglars stole two cash boxes containing 40 guilders and, worst of all, coupons for 330 pounds of sugar. Although, honestly, it could have been much worse.

Friday, July 23, 1943

Since you've never been through a war, Kitty, let me tell you, just for fun, what we each want to do first when we're able to go outside again.

Margot would love to stay in the bath for two days straight.

MORE PUDDING, MADEMOISELLE?

DO YOU HAVE A COPY OF <u>THE ODYSSEY</u>?

A LITTLE MORE PIANISSIMO, IF YOU COULD.

Madame van Daan longs for cake...

Just one cake...

Well... maybe more than one.

Mother is dying for a cup of real coffee.

Father would like to visit Mr. Voskuijl before he leaves us...

AH, OTTO, I'M AFRAID IT'S TOO LATE.

Peter would go out on the town.

And Dussel can think of nothing but seeing his Lotje...

As for me? I'd like to go back to school!

Monday, July 26, 1943

Dear Kitty, Yesterday was a very tumultuous day.

8:30 a.m.
The sirens woke me, flooding me with fear before I even opened my eyes.

9:00 a.m.–12:00 p.m.
Buried myself under the pillow.

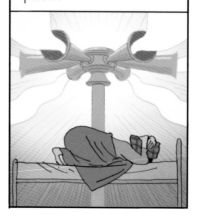

1:00 p.m.
Packed my escape bag—ready to run.

2:30 p.m.
Met Margot for some work in the office.

3:00 p.m.
Another siren.
The doorway felt like the only safe place.

4:00 p.m.
Clutched my escape bag again.

5:00 p.m.
Back to routine...

YOUR DAUGHTER IS LOSING TOUCH. SHE NEEDS TO GET A GRIP.

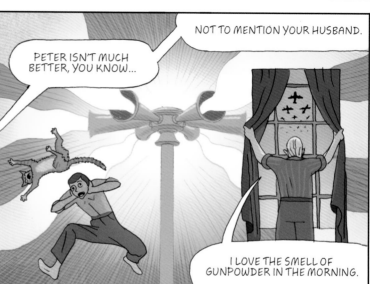

PETER ISN'T MUCH BETTER, YOU KNOW...

NOT TO MENTION YOUR HUSBAND.

I LOVE THE SMELL OF GUNPOWDER IN THE MORNING.

7:00 p.m.
Dinner was good, but I lost my appetite the moment I heard the siren.

9:00 p.m.
Here come the bombers again. I crawled into Father's bed.

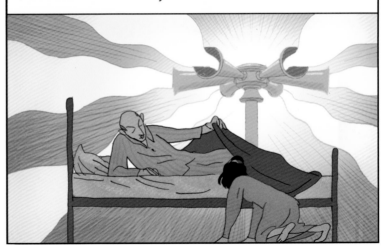

9:30 p.m.
Back to my room.

1:00 a.m.
The planes kept on coming.

1:00–2:00 a.m.

2:00 a.m.
Father carried me back to bed.

3:00–7:00 a.m.
Finally got some sleep.

7:30 a.m.
Morning: yet another round of planes.

Dear Kitty, Yesterday, Madame and Mr. Dussel were washing the dishes while I tried very hard not to start a fight.

YOU KNOW THAT BOOK YOU GAVE ME, MR. DUSSEL?

YES?...

WHAT AN UNBELIEVABLY STUPID BOOK IT WAS!

HOW DARE YOU!! YOU'RE AN OLD LADY IN THE BODY OF A CHILD!

EXACTLY! IN 20 YEARS, NOTHING WILL EXCITE YOU ANYMORE.

PLEASE, ANNE, JUST GIVE ME A CHANCE!

YOU'RE SO BORING...

I READ THIS DRIVEL 20 YEARS AGO.

THIS IS THE MOST BANAL WORK YOU'VE EVER COMPOSED, MR. SHOSTAKOVICH.

I WOULD SUGGEST, ANNE, THAT YOU MARRY SOMEONE RIGHT AWAY.

INDEED, 20 YEARS FROM NOW NO ONE WILL TAKE YOU.

Can you imagine how I felt?
That's when I decided to write my own book. It shall be called: <u>Madame van Daan</u>.

Madame van Daan was born in Germany many years ago. She was a sweet child.

BUY ME SWEETS! NOW!!!!

Then she grew up and became fond of boys.

She grew up some more and turned into a compulsive flirter. But only with strangers...

Then she immigrated to Holland. Daddy thinks that's where she became ugly.

Mother thinks that's when she became stupid.

I AM STILL A LADY, NO MATTER WHAT!

Margot thinks that's where she became unimportant.

And I think she's all of the above.

P.S. Will the reader please take into consideration that this story was written before the writer's fury had cooled?

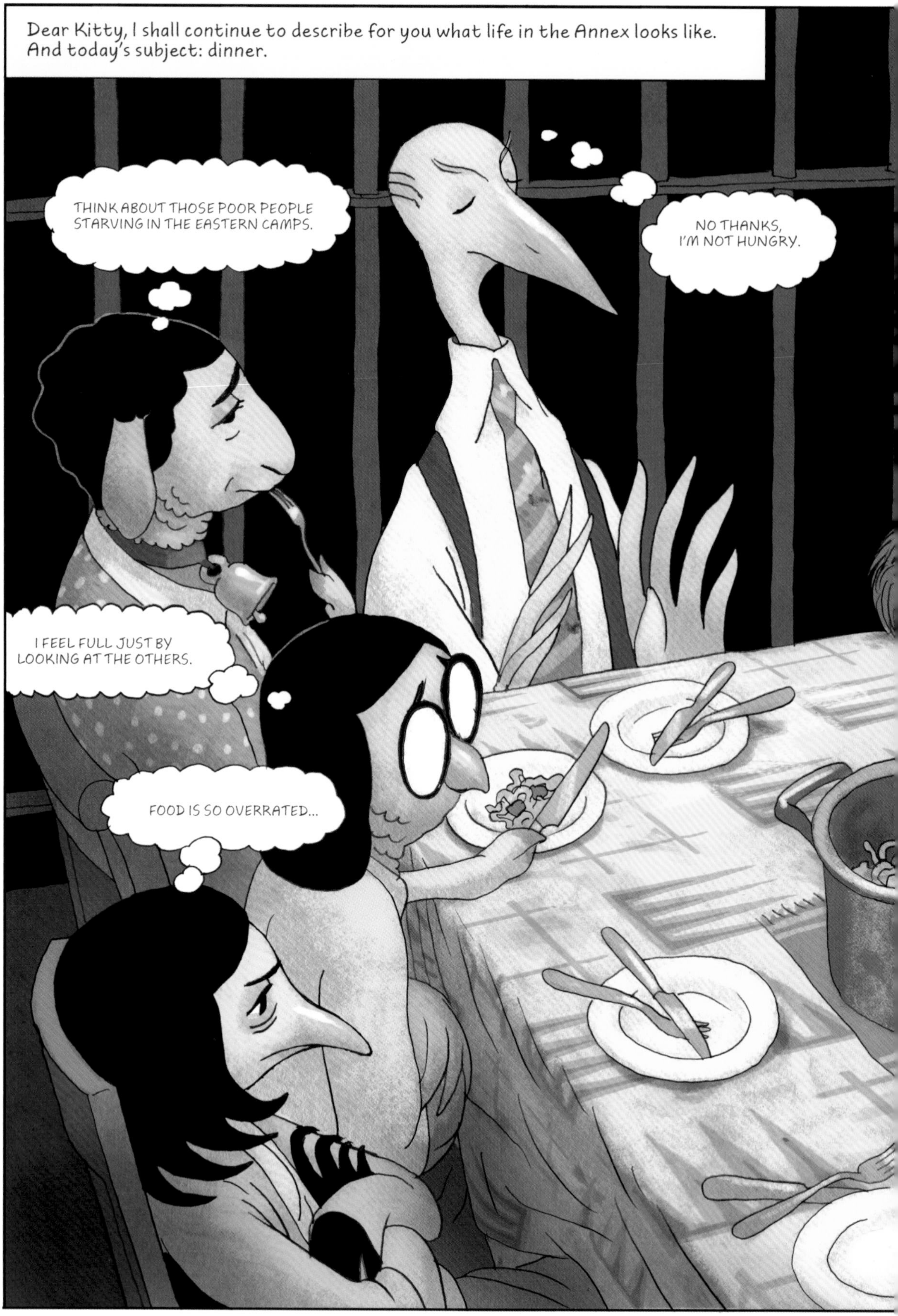
Dear Kitty, I shall continue to describe for you what life in the Annex looks like. And today's subject: dinner.
THINK ABOUT THOSE POOR PEOPLE STARVING IN THE EASTERN CAMPS.
NO THANKS, I'M NOT HUNGRY.
I FEEL FULL JUST BY LOOKING AT THE OTHERS.
FOOD IS SO OVERRATED...

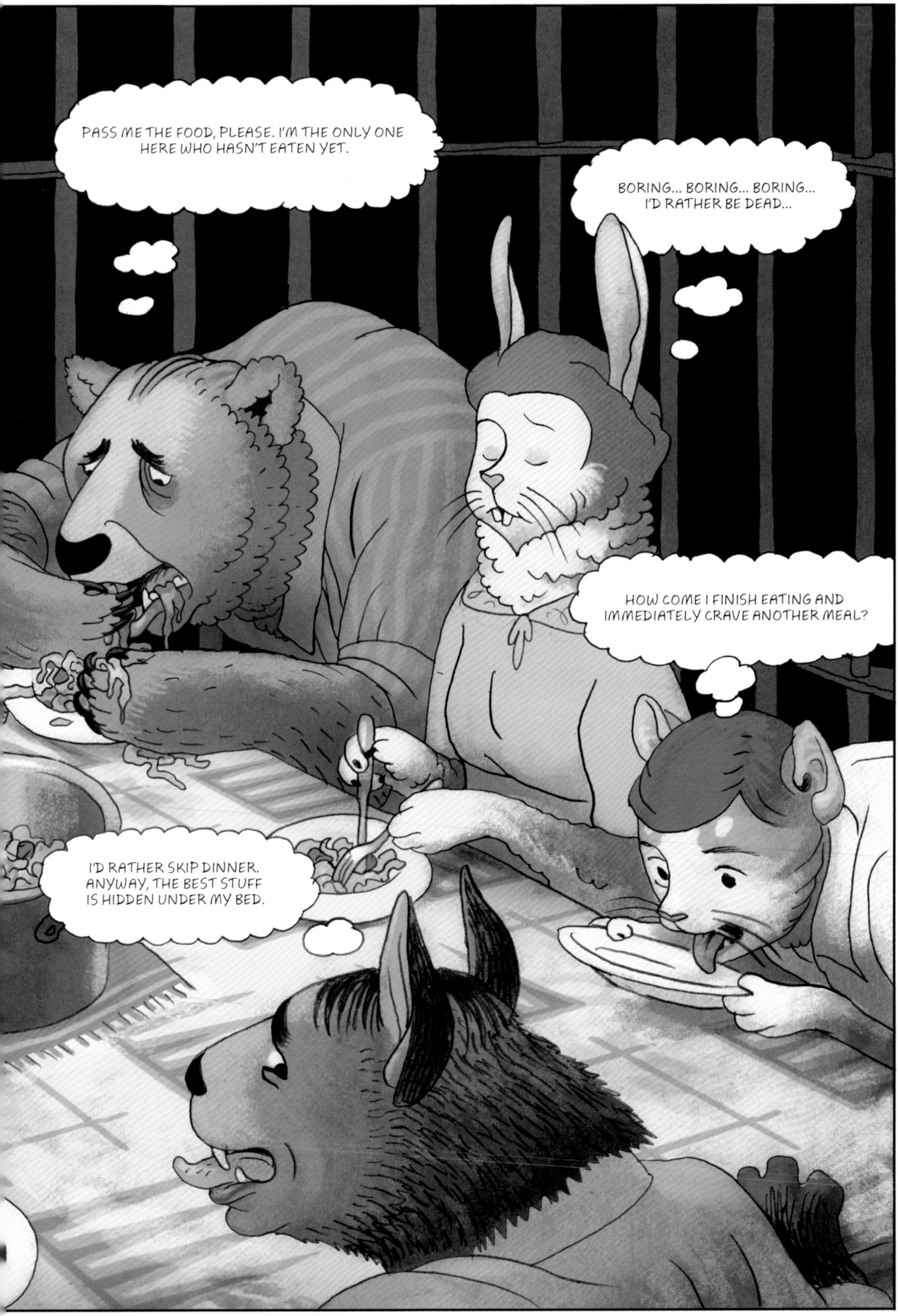
PASS ME THE FOOD, PLEASE. I'M THE ONLY ONE HERE WHO HASN'T EATEN YET.
BORING... BORING... BORING... I'D RATHER BE DEAD...
HOW COME I FINISH EATING AND IMMEDIATELY CRAVE ANOTHER MEAL?
I'D RATHER SKIP DINNER. ANYWAY, THE BEST STUFF IS HIDDEN UNDER MY BED.

Dear Kitty, Here is some of the best news of the war so far: Italy has capitulated! Unconditionally surrendered!

Who would have dreamed that even here in the Annex, we would pay a price for the Italian surrender?

PLEASE, MIEP, I BEG YOU, BRING ME THE BOOK ABOUT MUSSOLINI.

BUT YOU KNOW IT'S BANNED!

PRETTY PLEASE...?

WATCH OUT, THIS IS DANGEROUS STUFF—EXPLOSIVE.

On the way back to the Annex, Miep was hit by an SS motorcycle.

Just imagine what they would have done to her if they'd found the book.

Miep returned to the Annex injured.

With Miep out of commission, I think it's time to consider the dismal situation of our team of helpers. All of them are angels sent from heaven. That was how they looked when we entered the Annex.

But now Kleiman, our intelligence source and main supplier, has severe stomach problems. He is in and out of the hospital.

Voskuijl is practically dying.

His daughter Bep spends most of her time taking care of him.

Miep is stuck in the office because of the accident.

That leaves us with Mr. Kugler, who is up to his neck in work.

When I can't resist thinking about what will happen if our angels vanish, I plunge into deep sorrow.

Thursday, September 16, 1943

Dear Kitty, Mr. van Maaren, who works in the warehouse, keeps me awake at night with worries. He is suspicious, he asks too many questions, he's no fool, and he is cruel.

SAY, MIEP, HOW COME YOU GO TO THE LAB SO MANY TIMES A DAY?

THERE'S A BIG EXPERIMENT WE'RE DOING THERE.

HEY, BEP, I'VE BEEN WAITING FOR YOU FOR AGES! WHERE HAVE YOU BEEN?

UPSTAIRS.

UPSTAIRS? FOR GOD'S SAKE, WHAT WERE YOU DOING THERE FOR SO LONG?

HEY, MR. KUGLER, WHERE ARE YOU OFF TO?

THE DRUGSTORE NEXT DOOR.

Van Maaren was so suspicious that Mr. Kugler had to sneak up the stairs like a thief to visit us.

Only Mr. Kugler had a clever answer.

MR. KUGLER, I SUSPECT THAT MIEP, BEP, AND KLEIMAN HAVE A SECRET BUSINESS ON THE OTHER SIDE OF THE BUILDING.

NONSENSE! WE DON'T EVEN OWN THAT PART OF THE BUILDING.

At night, my obsessive thoughts about Mr. van Maaren turn into nightmares...

As you can see, I'm currently in the middle of a depression. I couldn't really tell you what set it off, but I think it stems from my cowardice, which confronts me at every turn.

I've been taking valerian every day to fight the anxiety and depression.

But even deep sleep brings no relief... The dreams still creep in.

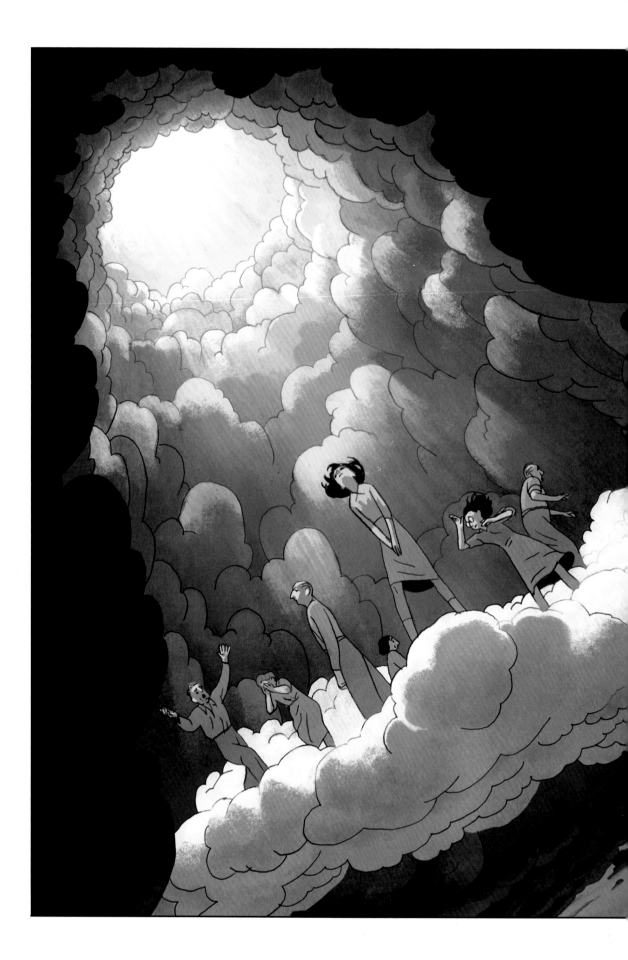

I simply can't imagine the world will ever be normal again for us. I do talk about "after the war," but it's as if I were talking about a castle in the air, something that can never come true.

I see the eight of us in the Annex as if we were a patch of blue sky surrounded by menacing black clouds. The perfectly round spot on which we're standing is still safe, but the clouds are moving in on us, and the ring between us and the approaching danger is being pulled tighter and tighter. We're surrounded by darkness and danger, and in our desperate search for a way out we keep bumping into each other.

We look at the fighting down below and the peace and beauty up above. In the meantime, we've been cut off by the dark mass of clouds, so that we can go neither up nor down. It looms before us like an impenetrable wall, trying to crush us, but not yet able to. I can only cry out and implore, "Oh, ring, ring, open wide and let us out!"

Dearest Kitty, The bad news is that the van Daans are broke. And they are raging!

WHERE?

PROBABLY IN THE WAREHOUSE.

THIS IS PROBABLY THE LAST CIGARETTE I'LL EVER SMOKE.

WHY IS THAT?

I LOST OUR LAST 100 GUILDERS...

Obviously the van Daans never thought how dangerous it would be if van Maaren starts trying to figure out where the money came from.

I SUGGEST YOU SELL YOUR SUIT, SINCE YOU CLEARLY DON'T NEED IT HERE.

OH, REALLY? I WONDER HOW MANY DEAD RABBITS ARE IN YOUR COAT! THEY'RE PROBABLY WORTH A FORTUNE.

HOW DARE YOU? SHE'S A LADY!

So first Mr. Kleiman tried to sell Hermann's suit...

Then it was Peter's bicycle...

And then the inevitable happened.

The entire Annex was on alert. We had the impression someone was definitely going to be killed upstairs...

All that bickering and nervous tension have become so stressful that I completely lost my appetite. So they're trying to plump me up...

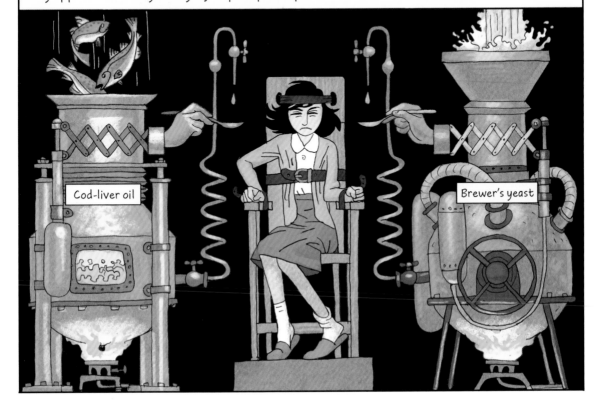

Cod-liver oil

Brewer's yeast

WHY ARE YOU READING MARGOT'S BOOK?

WHAT DO YOU CARE? SHE'S NOT EVEN HERE.

WELL, I'M HERE NOW—WHY ARE YOU READING MY BOOK?

CAN'T YOU JUST LET ME BE FOR ONE SECOND!

OH, ANNE, IMAGINE IF MARGOT HAD TAKEN YOUR BOOK.

I'M SO FED UP WITH YOU ALL!

OH, ANNE, YOU ARE SO CHILDISH.

It's not that I love only Father. I love Margot and Mother too, but only because they're Margot and Mother. I don't give a darn about them as people. As far as I'm concerned, they can go jump in the lake. It's different with Father. When I see him being partial to Margot, praising her, hugging her, I feel a gnawing ache inside, because I'm mad about him. I model myself on Father, and there's no one in the world I love more. It's a pity he doesn't realize that he treats Margot differently from me: Margot just happens to be

the cleverest

the kindest

the prettiest

the best!!!

But I have a right to be taken seriously too. I've always been the clown and mischief-maker of the family; I've always had to pay double for my sins: once with scoldings and then again with my own sense of despair. I'm no longer satisfied with the meaningless affection or the supposedly serious talks. I long for something from Father that he's incapable of giving. I'm not jealous of Margot; I never have been.

I'm not envious of her brains or her beauty. It's just that I'd like to feel that Father really loves me, not because I'm his child, but because I'm me, Anne. I cling to Father because my contempt of Mother is growing daily and it's only through him that I'm able to retain the last ounce of family feeling I have left. He doesn't understand that I sometimes need to vent my feelings for Mother. He doesn't want to talk about it, and he avoids any discussion involving Mother's failings.

And yet Mother, with all her shortcomings, is tougher for me to deal with. I don't know how I should behave. I can't very well confront her with her carelessness, her sarcasm, and her hard-heartedness, yet I can't continue to take the blame for everything. I'm the opposite of Mother, so of course we clash. I don't mean to judge her; I don't have that right. I'm simply looking at her as a mother. She's not a mother to me—I have to mother myself.

I've cut myself adrift from them. I'm charting my own course, and we'll see where it leads me. I have no choice, because I can picture what a mother and a wife should be and can't seem to find anything of the sort in the woman I'm supposed to call "Mother." I tell myself time and again to overlook Mother's bad example. I only want to see her good points, and to look inside myself for what's lacking in her.

But it doesn't work, and the worst part is that Father and Mother don't realize their own inadequacies and how much I blame them for letting me down. Are there any parents who can make their children completely happy? Sometimes I think God is trying to test me, both now and in the future. I'll have to become a good person on my own, without anyone to serve as a model or advise me, but it'll make me stronger in the end. Who else but me is ever going to read these letters? Who else but me can I turn to for comfort? I'm frequently in need of consolation, I often feel weak, and more often than not, I fail to meet expectations. I know this, and every day I resolve to do better.

They aren't consistent in their treatment of me. One day they say that Anne's a sensible girl and entitled to know everything, and the next that Anne's a silly goose who doesn't know a thing and yet imagines she's learned all she needs to know from books! I'm no longer the baby and spoiled little darling whose every deed can be laughed at. I have my own ideas, plans, and ideals, but am unable to articulate them yet.

Oh well. So much comes into my head at night, when I'm alone, or during the day, when I'm obliged to put up with people I can't abide or who invariably misinterpret my intentions. That's why I always come back to my diary—I start there and end there because Kitty's always patient. I promise her that, despite everything, I'll keep going, that I'll find my own way and choke back my tears. I only wish I could see some results or, just once, receive encouragement from someone who loves me. Don't condemn me, but think of me as a person who sometimes reaches bursting point!

Yours, Anne

Dear Kitty, Last night, just as I was falling asleep, Hanneli Goslar appeared before me.

OH, ANNE, WHY HAVE YOU DESERTED ME?

RESCUE ME FROM THIS HELL, PLEASE!

To be honest, I hadn't thought of Hanneli for months—no, for at least a year. I feel such shame: I am here with everything I could wish for, while she is dying out there...

Now Hanneli's eyes haunt me, whatever I do and wherever I go.

Wednesday, December 22, 1943

Dear Kitty, A bad case of flu has prevented me from writing to you for a long time.

I had to cough under the blanket... so the Nazis wouldn't hear me.

I tried milk with honey and raw egg.

Steam.

Wet compresses.

Dry compresses.

Hot water bottle.

The worst part was when Mr. Dussel suddenly remembered he was actually a doctor.

Thank God we had the double excitement of Hanukkah and Christmas, with lots of presents from our saviors.

Thursday, December 30, 1943

Dearest Kitty, Just as we thought things had settled down here, dark thunderclouds are heading this way, and all because of food.

WHY DON'T WE FRY ALL THE POTATOES IN THE MORNING AND SAVE HALF OF THEM TO EAT IN THE AFTERNOON?

WE FRANKS DO NOT EAT COLD, SOGGY VEGETABLES!

Next thing you know, after 15 months in the Annex, we decided to split all the food in half.

13... 14... 15

CAN WE HAVE THE SLICES WITH MORE FAT?

ABSOLUTELY, WE DON'T EAT FAT.

Even the sugar...

If only we could split completely from the van Daans!

Wishful thinking...

Sunday, January 2, 1944

Dearest Kitty,

This morning, when I had nothing to do, I leafed through the pages of my diary and came across so many letters dealing with the subject of "Mother" in such strong terms that I was shocked. I said to myself, "Anne, is that really you talking about hate? Oh, Anne, how could you?"

I continued to sit with the open book in my hand and wonder why I was filled with so much anger and hate that I had to confide it all to you. I tried to understand the Anne of last year and make apologies for her, because as long as I leave you with these accusations and don't attempt to explain what prompted them, my conscience won't be clear.

I was suffering then (and still do) from moods that kept my head under water (figuratively speaking) and allowed me to see things only from my own perspective, without calmly considering what the others—those whom I, with my mercurial temperament, had hurt or offended—had said, and then behaving as they would have done. I hid inside myself, thought of no one but myself, and calmly wrote down all my joy, sarcasm, and sorrow in my diary. Because this diary has become a kind of scrapbook, it means a great deal to me, but I could easily write "over and done with" on many of its pages.

I was furious at Mother (and still am a lot of the time).

It's true, she didn't understand me, but I didn't understand her either. Because she loved me, she was tender and affectionate, but because of the difficult situations I put her in, and the sad circumstances in which she found herself, she was nervous and irritable, so I can understand why she was often short with me. I was offended, took it far too much to heart, and was insolent and beastly to her, which, in turn, made her unhappy. We were caught in a vicious circle of unpleasantness and sorrow. Not a very happy period for either of us, but at least it's coming to an end. I didn't want to see what was going on, and I felt very sorry for myself, but that's understandable too.

Those violent outbursts on paper are simply expressions of anger that, in normal life, I could have worked off by locking myself in my room and stamping my foot a few times or calling Mother names behind her back. The period of tearfully passing judgment on Mother is over. I've grown wiser and Mother's nerves are a bit steadier.

Most of the time I manage to hold my tongue when I'm annoyed, and she does too; so, on the surface, we seem to be getting along better.

But there's one thing I can't do, and that's to love Mother with the devotion of a child.

I soothe my conscience with the thought that it's better for unkind words to be down on paper than for Mother to have to carry them around in her heart.

Yours, Anne

89

Thursday, January 6, 1944

Dearest Kitty, Yesterday I read an article about blushing. It was as if she'd addressed it directly to me.

During puberty girls withdraw into themselves and begin to think about the wondrous changes taking place in their bodies.

Whenever I have my period, I have the feeling that in spite of all the pain and discomfort, I'm carrying around a sweet secret.

EVERYTHING ALL RIGHT?

WHY THE SMILE, ANNE?

EVERYTHING IS LOVELY, THANKS FOR ASKING.

But I had these feelings even before my period...
I remember particularly one time when I spent the night at Jacque's.

UM... JACQUE... COULD WE SHOW EACH OTHER OUR BREASTS?

WHY?

AS PROOF OF OUR FRIENDSHIP.

ABSOLUTELY NOT!

If only she had known my terrible desire to kiss her...

90

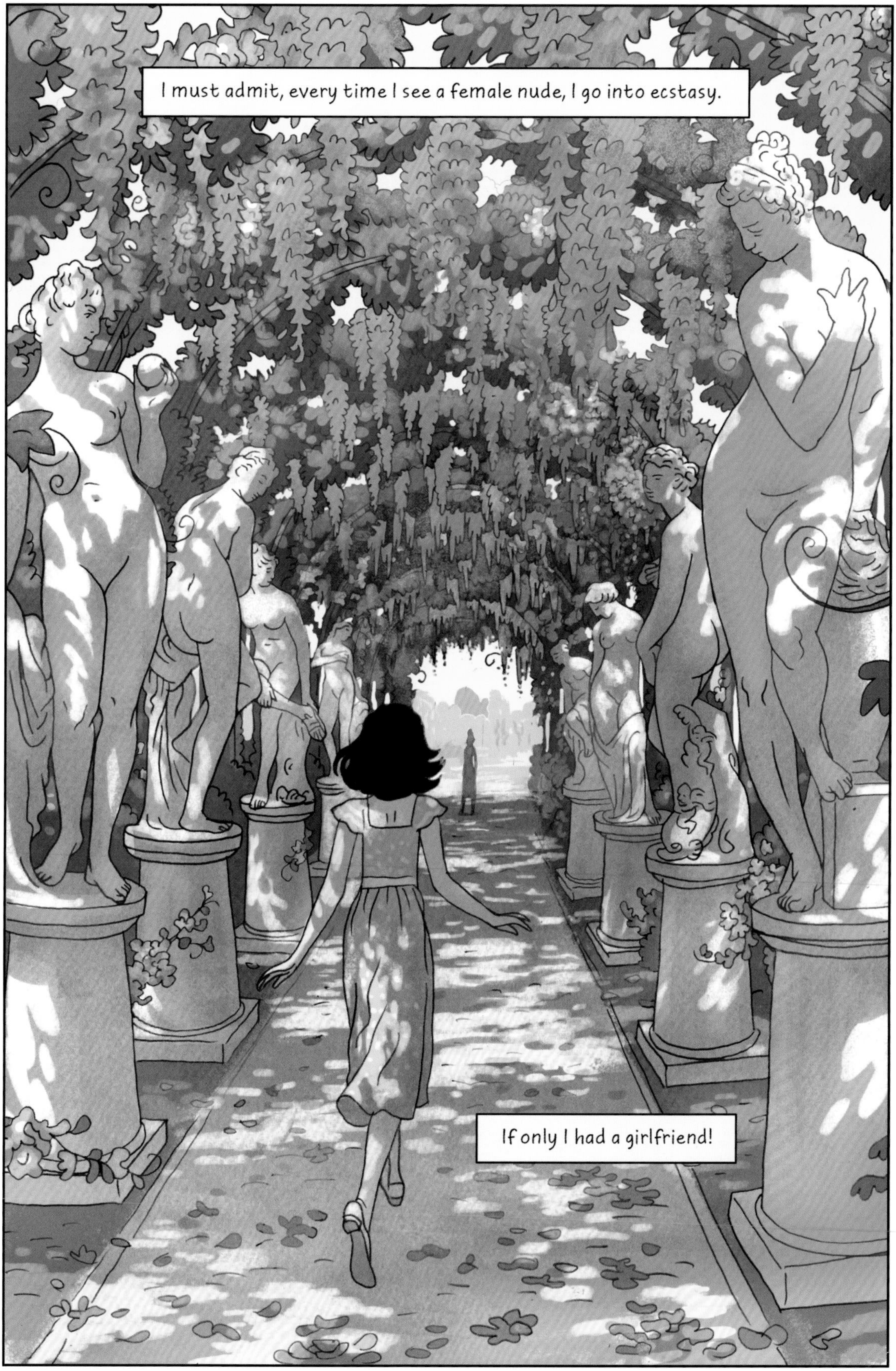
I must admit, every time I see a female nude, I go into ecstasy.
If only I had a girlfriend!

Thursday, January 6, 1944

Dearest Kitty, My longing to talk to someone has become unbearable.

PETER??

COME IN, PLEASE. MAYBE YOU COULD HELP ME?

WOW! I'VE BEEN LOOKING FOR THAT PIECE FOR AGES...

I wanted to say: How come I never noticed how deep and beautiful your eyes are? How come I didn't see how gentle and sensitive you are?

But instead, I said:

I RECENTLY READ THIS ARTICLE ABOUT BLUSHING...

UMMM...

AND... UMMM...

...WELL... UMMM... THE AUTHOR WRITES THAT ACTUALLY MEN START BLUSHING ONCE THEY START THINKING ABOUT THEIR PUBERTY PROCESS, AND EVERYTHING THAT GOES WITH IT...

THANK GOD YOUNG WOMEN DO NOT BLUSH AT ALL.

That night, I dreamed that Peter and I were gazing at the original painting from the puzzle in a famous museum.

And then he turned to me...

I MISSED YOU SO MUCH, MY LITTLE ANNE...

But it was not Peter van Daan... it was my old love, Petel. He had come for a visit, to remind me what true love is...

Dearest Kitty, After dreaming about my Petel, I woke up in an utter state of confusion.

DEAREST, WHAT A LOVELY SMILE THIS MORNING!

If Father only knew who I was thinking about.

IS THAT ME?

CLEAR EYES

ROSY CHEEKS

Then I imagined me and Petel together, crying...

...and it happened!

Kitty, I feel like such an idiot. I forgot that I haven't yet told you the history of my love life.

As a little girl, I took a liking to Sally Kimmel.

He was a sweet, chubby, funny boy.

FRRRRT

Until one day...

WHO'S THAT, SALLY?

THAT'S MY COUSIN APPY.

Appy and I, we were inseparable.

But he started looking like a matinee idol...

Thank God, Petel arrived.

HEY, SWEETIE, CAN I WALK YOU TO SCHOOL?

I was Petel's sweetheart for many months.

I'M GOING ON VACATION, SWEETIE. WAIT FOR ME!

When he came back, he was a man, but I was still a child.

It takes a long time for the heart to heal.

And a little war helps the process along...

My heart recovered with a new Peter.

Monday, January 24, 1944

Dear Kitty, Before I came here, whenever anyone at home or at school talked about sex, they were either secretive or disgusting.

DID YOU SEE WHAT A PAIR OF MELONS SHE'S SPROUTED?!

OH, ANNE, HOW COULD YOU!

AND THEN HE WAS JUST ALL OVER HER...!

OH, ANNE, I CAN'T BELIEVE YOU WOULD SAY THAT!

IT'S ONLY A MOVIE, MARGOT.

NEVER EVER DISCUSS IT WITH BOYS. AND IF THEY BRING IT UP, JUST IGNORE THEM.

This is why I was so surprised when the conversation somehow turned to Boche's sex, while the three of us were peeling potatoes.

BOCHE IS SO FAT. WHEN IS SHE GOING TO HAVE KITTENS?

BUT BOCHE IS A TOMCAT!

A PREGNANT TOMCAT...?

DON'T BELIEVE ME? COME AND SEE FOR YOURSELF.

Margot couldn't care less or maybe she was too embarrassed, so I went with Peter to the attic to check out Boche's sexual organs.

ISN'T HE SUPPOSED TO HAVE TESTICLES?

THEY REMOVED THEM, BUT HE STILL HAS HIS SEXUAL ORGAN.

WERE YOU THERE?

OF COURSE, I HELD HIS PAW.

PETER, WHY DO YOU CALL IT A SEXUAL ORGAN? DON'T THESE THINGS HAVE NAMES?

SUCH AS...?

VAGINA.

VAGINA? I SEE WHAT YOU MEAN... THE EQUIVALENT OF VAGINA...? I'LL ASK MY MOTHER.

MOM?!

Only at dinner did I realize: yes, it really did happen! Such an amazing discussion with Peter. I'd never have talked to a girl about this in such a normal tone of voice. I'm also certain that this isn't what Mother meant when she warned me about boys.

All the same, I wasn't exactly my usual self for the rest of the day. When I thought back to our talk, it struck me as odd. But I've learned at least one thing: there are young people, even those of the opposite sex, who can discuss these things naturally, without cracking jokes.

PENIS.

Friday, January 28, 1944

Life in the Annex has become very harsh recently. But I haven't given up my passion for cinema and film-stars.

HERE YOU GO, ANNE. LET ME TELL YOU, IT'S A RARE FIND, THESE DAYS.

Cinema & Theater

10,

I read all the reviews, I know all the plots of the leading films by heart, and the entire cast of course. I love to sail in with a new hairstyle, inspired by my beloved actresses.

Bette Davis

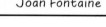

Joan Fontaine

Carole Lombard

Katharine Hepburn

Ingrid Bergman

Marlene Dietrich

98

As for you, my beloved Kitty, I was wondering whether you ever felt like a cow, having to chew my stale news over and over and over again. I am sure it is unbearable for you, Kitty. The grown-ups have the habit of repeating their stories again and again, and it all boils down to this: whenever one of the eight of us opens his mouth, the other seven can finish the story for him.

The papers are all full of invasion news and it's driving everyone insane. In the event of a British landing in Holland, they say the Germans will do anything to prevent it, even flood the country. They've published maps of Holland showing potential flooded areas. Our neighborhood is sure to be flooded. We'll have to swim...

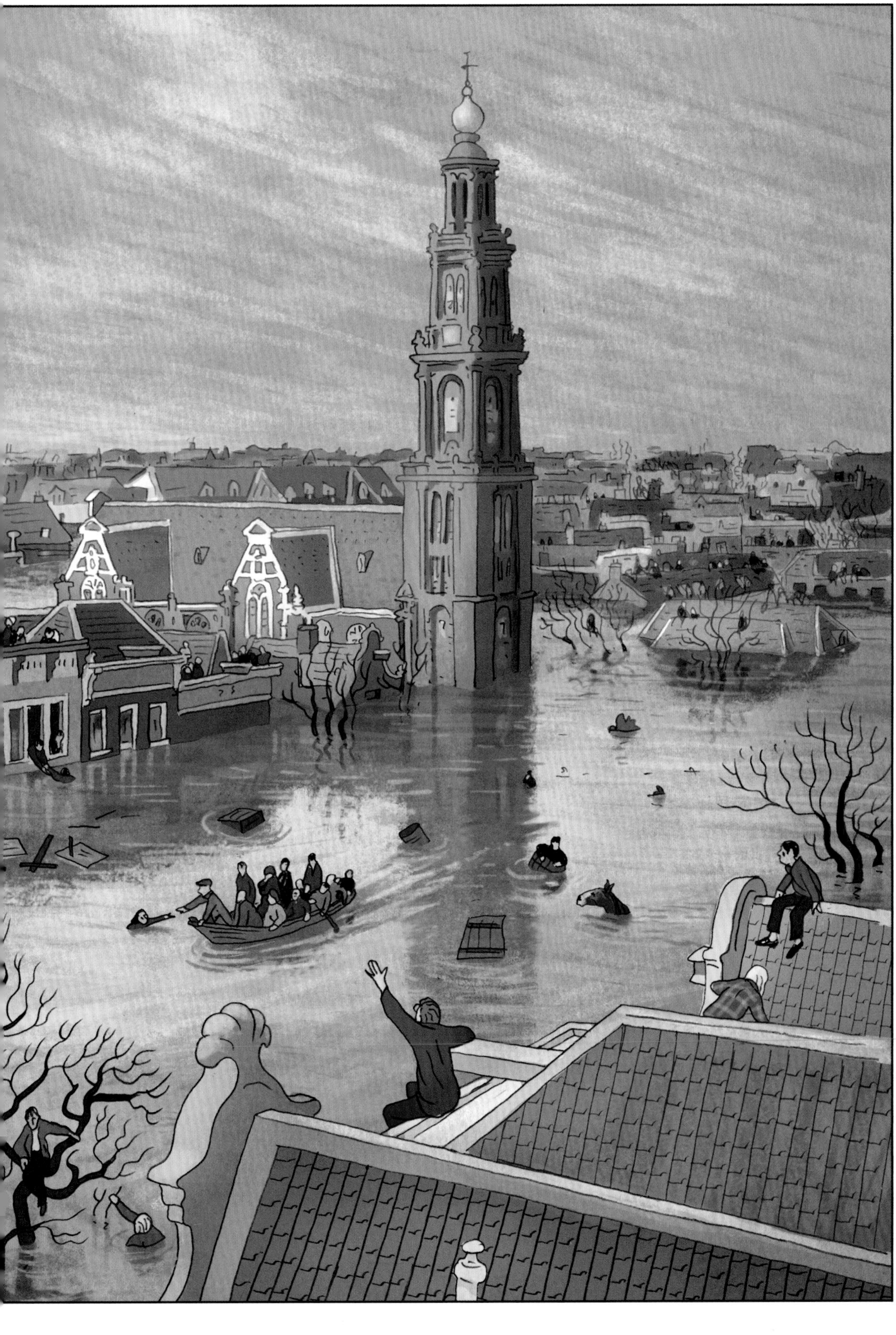

Tuesday, February 8, 1944

Dear Kitty,

As I seem to be going through a period of reflection at the moment and letting my mind range over anything and everything, my thoughts have naturally turned to Father and Mother's marriage. It has always been presented to me as an ideal marriage. Never a quarrel, no angry faces, perfect harmony, etc., etc.

I know a few things about Father's past, and what I don't know, I've made up; I have the impression that Father married Mother because he felt she would be a suitable wife. I have to admit I admire Mother for the way she assumed the role of his wife and has never, as far as I know, complained or been jealous. It can't be easy for a loving wife to know she'll never be first in her husband's affections, and Mother did know that. Father certainly admired Mother's attitude and thought she had an excellent character. Why marry anyone else? His ideals had been shattered and his youth was over. What kind of marriage has it turned out to be?

No quarrels or differences of opinion—but hardly an ideal marriage. Father respects Mother and loves her, but not with the kind of love I envision for a marriage. Father accepts Mother as she is, is often annoyed, but says as little as possible, because he knows the sacrifices Mother has had to make.

Father doesn't always ask her opinion—about the business, about other matters, about people, about all kinds of things.

He doesn't tell her everything, because he knows she's far too emotional, far too critical, and often far too biased. Father's not in love. He kisses her the way he kisses us. He never holds her up as an example, because he can't. He looks at her teasingly, or mockingly, but never lovingly. It may be that Mother's great sacrifice has made her harsh and disagreeable toward those around her, but it's guaranteed to take her even further from the path of love, to arouse even less admiration, and one day Father is bound to realize that while, on the outside, she has never demanded his total love, on the inside, she has slowly but surely been crumbling away. She loves him more than anyone, and it's hard to see this kind of love not being returned.

So should I actually feel more sympathy for Mother? Should I help her? And Father?— I can't, I'm always imagining another mother. I just can't.—How could I? She hasn't told me anything about herself, and I've never asked her to. What do we know of each other's thoughts? I can't talk to her, I can't look lovingly into those cold eyes, I can't. Not ever!—If she had even one quality an understanding mother is supposed to have, gentleness or friendliness or patience or something, I'd keep trying to get closer to her. But as for loving this insensitive person, this mocking creature—it's becoming more and more impossible every day!

Yours, Anne

Monday, February 14, 1944

Dear Kitty, On Sunday morning I noticed, to my great joy (I'll be honest with you), that Peter kept looking at me. Not in a casual way but in a very different, sensitive way.

When he was not looking at me, I had to look at him.

CAN YOU PLEASE HELP ME FIND SOME REALLY SMALL POTATOES?

WHY?

FOR MARGOT'S BIRTHDAY.

THESE ARE NOT ELEGANT ENOUGH.

YOU KNOW, I ENVY YOU TERRIBLY, ANNE.

ME?

THE WAY YOU EXPRESS YOUR FEELINGS...

AS A BOY, WHENEVER I WAS ANGRY AT SOMEONE...

...I'D BEAT THEM UP.

NOW I CAN'T BEAT ANYONE UP ANYMORE, AND MY TONGUE IS TIED. I WISH I STILL HAD THAT OLD HABIT.

DON'T YOU EVER CHANGE THE STATION AGAIN!

OH, YOU'RE WRONG ABOUT ME, PETER. MOST OF WHAT I SAY COMES OUT TOO LONG AND TACTLESS.

MAYBE, BUT YOU NEVER SEEM TO LOOK EMBARRASSED.

WELL, PETER... IF YOU SAY SO...

Wednesday, February 23, 1944

This morning, as I did every morning, I woke up and went straight to Peter's attic.

I sat silently on my usual spot on the floor.

Peter came to sit beside me.

We didn't have to say a single word, it was so perfect: just us and nature.

The world didn't exist.

P.S. Thoughts: To Peter.

We've been missing out on so much here, so very much, and for such a long time. I miss it just as much as you do. I'm not talking about external things, since we're well provided for in that sense; I mean the internal things. Like you, I long for freedom and fresh air, but I think we've been amply compensated for their loss. On the inside, I mean. This morning, when I was sitting in front of the window and taking a long, deep look outside at God and nature, I was happy, just plain happy. Peter, as long as people feel that kind of happiness within themselves, the joy of nature, health, and much more besides, they'll always be able to recapture that happiness.

Riches, prestige, everything can be lost. But the happiness in your own heart can only be dimmed; it will always be there, as long as you live, to make you happy again. Whenever you're feeling lonely or sad, try going to the loft on a beautiful day and looking outside. Not at the houses and the rooftops, but at the sky. As long as you can look fearlessly at the sky, you'll know that you're pure within and will find happiness once more.

My dearest Kitty,

It's like a nightmare, one that goes on long after I'm awake. I see him nearly every hour of the day and yet I can't be with him, I can't let the others notice, and I have to pretend to be cheerful, though my heart is aching. As if that is not enough, Peter Schiff and Peter van Daan have melted into one Peter, who's good and kind and whom I long for desperately. I'm sentimental, I know. I'm despondent and foolish, I know that too.

Oh, help me!

Yours, Anne M. Frank

Dearest Kitty, When I think back to my life it all seems so unreal.

The Anne Frank who enjoyed that heavenly existence was completely different from the one who has grown wise within these walls.

1942

I had five admirers following me wherever I went.

ME!

ME!

ME!

ME!

ME!

SO, WHICH ONE OF YOU BOYS IS GOING TO TAKE ME TO THE MOVIES TONIGHT?

YOU DIDN'T TELL ME YOU WERE BRINGING ALL YOUR FRIENDS ALONG!

IT'S NOT ALL MY FRIENDS: ONLY MY 20 BEST FRIENDS.

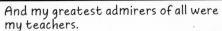

And my greatest admirers of all were my teachers.

THE MOST ASTONISHING FACT IS THAT NAPOLEON USED TO WEAR SILK UNDERWEAR!

THIS IS SO BRILLIANT OF YOU, ANNE. WHERE ON EARTH DID YOU FIND THIS INFORMATION?

I'd made it all up, of course, but I was so charming, such a flirt, that no one could resist me!

Would all that admiration eventually have made me overconfident? I wonder what they really thought about me back then in school.

In spite of everything, I wasn't altogether happy in 1942; I often felt I'd been deserted, but because I was on the go all day long, I didn't think about it. I enjoyed myself as much as I could, trying consciously or unconsciously to fill the void with jokes. After coming to the Annex, it took me more than a year to get used to doing without admiration. I look back at that Anne Frank, only two years ago, and I realize that this period of my life has irrevocably come to a close; my happy-go-lucky, carefree school days are gone forever. I don't even miss them. I've outgrown them. I can no longer just be frivolous, since my serious side is always there.

I also discovered an inner happiness underneath my superficial and cheerful exterior. Now I live only for Peter, since what happens to me in the future depends largely on him! I lie in bed at night, after saying my prayers, and I'm filled with joy. I think of going into hiding, Peter's love (which is still so new and fragile and which neither of us dares to say aloud), the future, happiness and love as the world, nature and the tremendous beauty of everything, all that splendor. At such moments I don't think about all the misery, but about the beauty that still remains.

Mother's method for fighting melancholy.

My method for fighting melancholy.

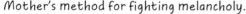

This is where Mother and I differ greatly.

Her advice in the face of melancholy is: "Think about all the suffering in the world and be thankful you're not part of it." My advice is: "Go outside, to the country, enjoy the sun and all nature has to offer. Go outside and try to recapture the happiness within yourself; think of all the beauty in yourself and in everything around you, and be happy." I don't think Mother's advice can be right, because what are you supposed to do if you become part of the suffering? You'll be completely lost. On the contrary, beauty remains, even in misfortune. If you just look for it, you discover more and more happiness and regain your balance. A person who's happy will make others happy; a person who has courage and faith will never die in misery!

Yours, Anne M. Frank

Wednesday, March 8, 1944

Two nights ago I dreamed I was skating here in the living room, with that little boy from the Apollo skating rink and his spindly-legged sister.

HI, I'M PETER. WHO ARE YOU?

When I approached him, I suddenly realized he wasn't who I thought he was.

Next thing I knew, we were in the attic, kissing passionately.

DO YOU LOVE ME?

NO, I DON'T LOVE YOU, NOT AT ALL.

When I woke up in a sweat, I was glad Peter hadn't said that after all.

But Peter's cheeks were very disappointing: they were more like Father's—the cheeks of a man who already shaves.

The people who supply us with food coupons have been arrested, and our special black market agent, Mr. M., was captured by the Germans in a violent raid on the black market.

The food is wretched. The kitchen smells like a mixture of spoiled plums, rotten eggs, and brine.

The potatoes are diseased—I think it's cancer, which requires immediate surgery.

Coming soon: starvation.

Monday, March 20, 1944

Dearest Kitty,

Lately, a shadow has fallen on my happiness. For a long time I've had the feeling that Margot likes Peter.

Just how much I don't know, but the whole situation is very unpleasant. Now every time I go and see Peter I'm hurting her, without meaning to. The funny thing is that she hardly lets it show. I know I'd be insanely jealous, but Margot just says I shouldn't feel sorry for her.

"I think it's so awful that you've become the odd one out," I told her.

"I'm used to that," she replied, somewhat bitterly.

But then there came evidence of Margot's goodness. This letter came a few hours after our conversation:

Anne,

Yesterday, when I said I wasn't jealous of you, I wasn't being entirely honest. The situation is this: I'm not jealous of either you or Peter.

I'm just sorry I haven't found anyone with whom to share my thoughts and feelings, and I'm not likely to in the near future. But that's why I wish, from the bottom of my heart, that you will both be able to place your trust in each other. You're already missing out on so much here, things other people take for granted.

On the other hand, I'm certain I'd never have got as far with Peter, because I think I'd need to feel very close to a person before I could share my thoughts. I'd want to have the feeling that he understood me through and through, even if I didn't say much. For this reason it would have to be someone I felt was intellectually superior to me, and that isn't the case with Peter. But I can imagine your feeling close to him. So there's no need for you to reproach yourself because you think you're taking something I was entitled to; nothing could be further from the truth. You and Peter have everything to gain by your friendship.

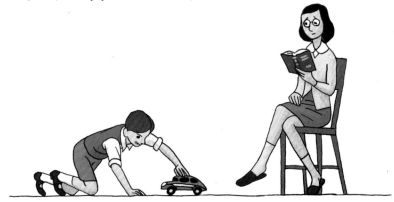

My answer:

Dearest Margot,

Your letter was extremely kind, but I still don't feel completely happy about the situation, and I don't think I ever will.

At the moment, Peter and I don't trust each other as much as you seem to think. It's just that when you're standing beside an open window at twilight, you can say more to each other than in bright sunshine. It's also easier to whisper your feelings than to shout them from the rooftops. I think you've begun to feel a kind of sisterly affection for Peter and would like to help him, just as much as I would.

Perhaps you'll be able to do that someday, though that's not the kind of trust we have in mind. I believe that trust has to come from both sides. If there's anything you still want to discuss, please write, because it's easier for me to say what I mean on paper than face-to-face.

You know how much I admire you, and only hope that some of your goodness and Father's goodness will rub off on me, because, in that sense, you two are a lot alike.

Yours, Anne

This was Margot's answer:

Dear Anne,

After your letter of yesterday I have the unpleasant feeling that your conscience bothers you whenever you go to Peter's to work or talk; there's really no reason for that. In my heart, I know there's someone who deserves my trust (as I do his), and I wouldn't be able to tolerate Peter in his place.

However, as you wrote, I do think of Peter as a kind of brother... a younger brother; we've been sending out feelers, and a brotherly and sisterly affection may or may not develop at some later date, but it's certainly not reached that stage yet.

So there's no need for you to feel sorry for me.

Now that you've found companionship, enjoy it as much as you can.

Yours,
Margot

Yesterday a plane crashed nearby. The crew was able to parachute out in time. It crashed on top of a school. There was a small fire and a couple of people were killed. As the airmen made their descent, the Germans sprayed them with bullets. The Amsterdammers who saw it seethed with rage at such a dastardly deed. We—by which I mean the ladies—were also scared out of our wits. Brrr, I hate the sound of gunfire.

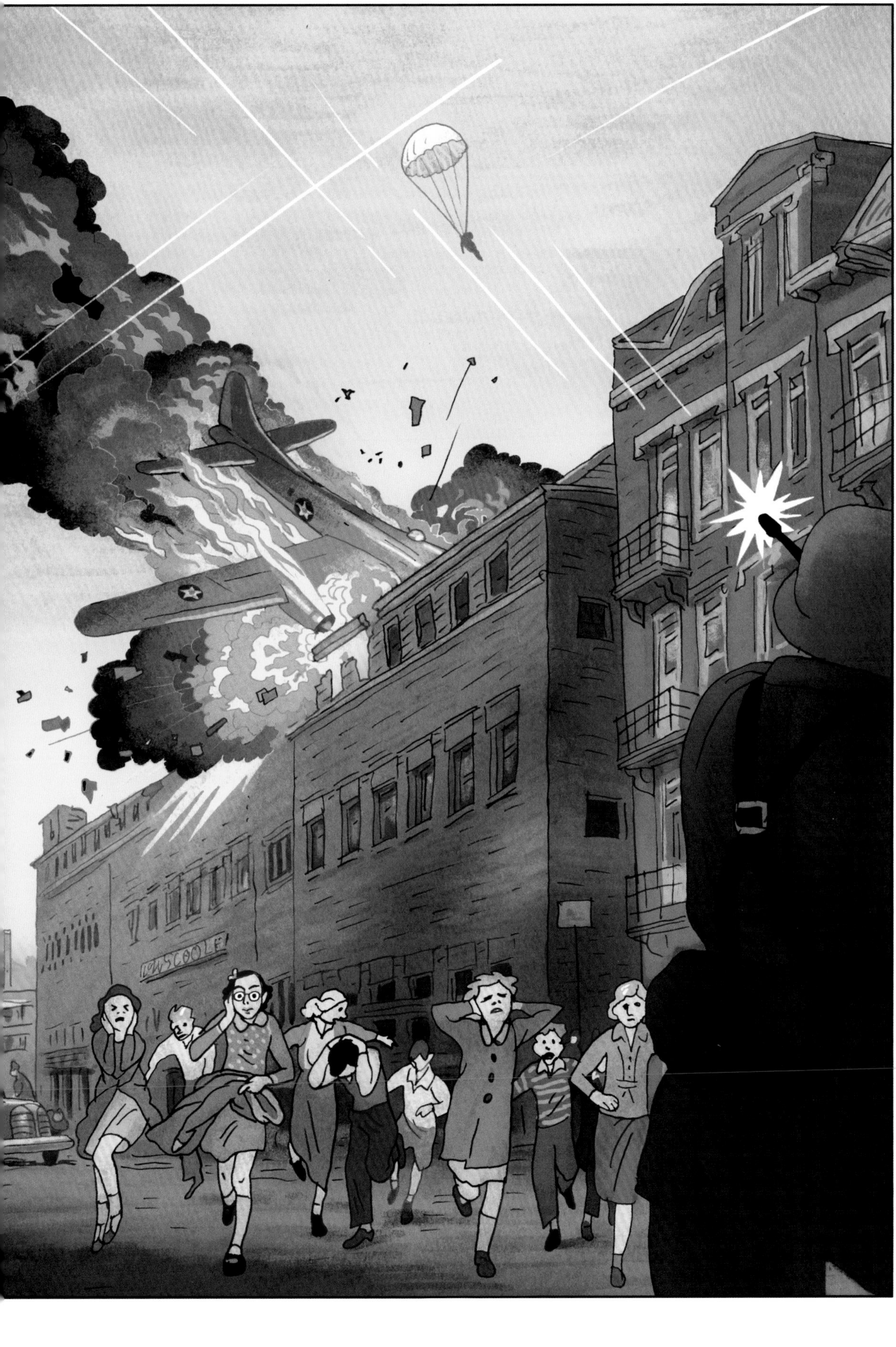

I'd like to ask Peter whether he knows what girls look like down there. I don't think boys are as complicated as girls. You can easily see what boys look like in photographs or pictures of male nudes, but with women it's different. In women, the genitals, or whatever they're called, are hidden between their legs. Peter has probably never seen a girl up close. To tell you the truth, neither have I. Boys are a lot easier. How on earth would I go about describing a girl's parts? I can tell from what he said that he doesn't know exactly how it all fits together. He was talking about the "Muttermund,"* but that's on the inside, where you can't see it. Everything's pretty well arranged in us women. Until I was eleven or twelve, I didn't realize there was a second set of labia on the inside, since you couldn't see them. What's even funnier is that I thought urine came out of the clitoris. I asked Mother once what that little bump was, and she said she didn't know. She can really play dumb when she wants to!

But to get back to the subject. How on earth can you explain what it all looks like without any models? Shall I try anyway? Okay, here goes!

When you're standing up, all you see from the front is hair. Between your legs there are two soft, cushiony things, also covered with hair, which press together when you're standing, so you can't see what's inside. They separate when you sit down, and they're very red and quite fleshy on the inside. In the upper part, between the outer labia, there's a fold of skin that, on second thought, looks like a kind of blister. That's the clitoris. Then come the inner labia, which are also pressed together in a kind of crease. When they open up, you can see a fleshy little mound, no bigger than the top of my thumb. The upper part has a couple of small holes in it, which is where the urine comes out. The lower part looks as if it were just skin, and yet that's where the vagina is. You can barely find it, because the folds of skin hide the opening. The hole's so small I can hardly imagine how a man could get in there, much less how a baby could come out. It's hard enough trying to get your index finger inside. That's all there is, and yet it plays such an important role!

Yours, Anne M. Frank

*Cervix.

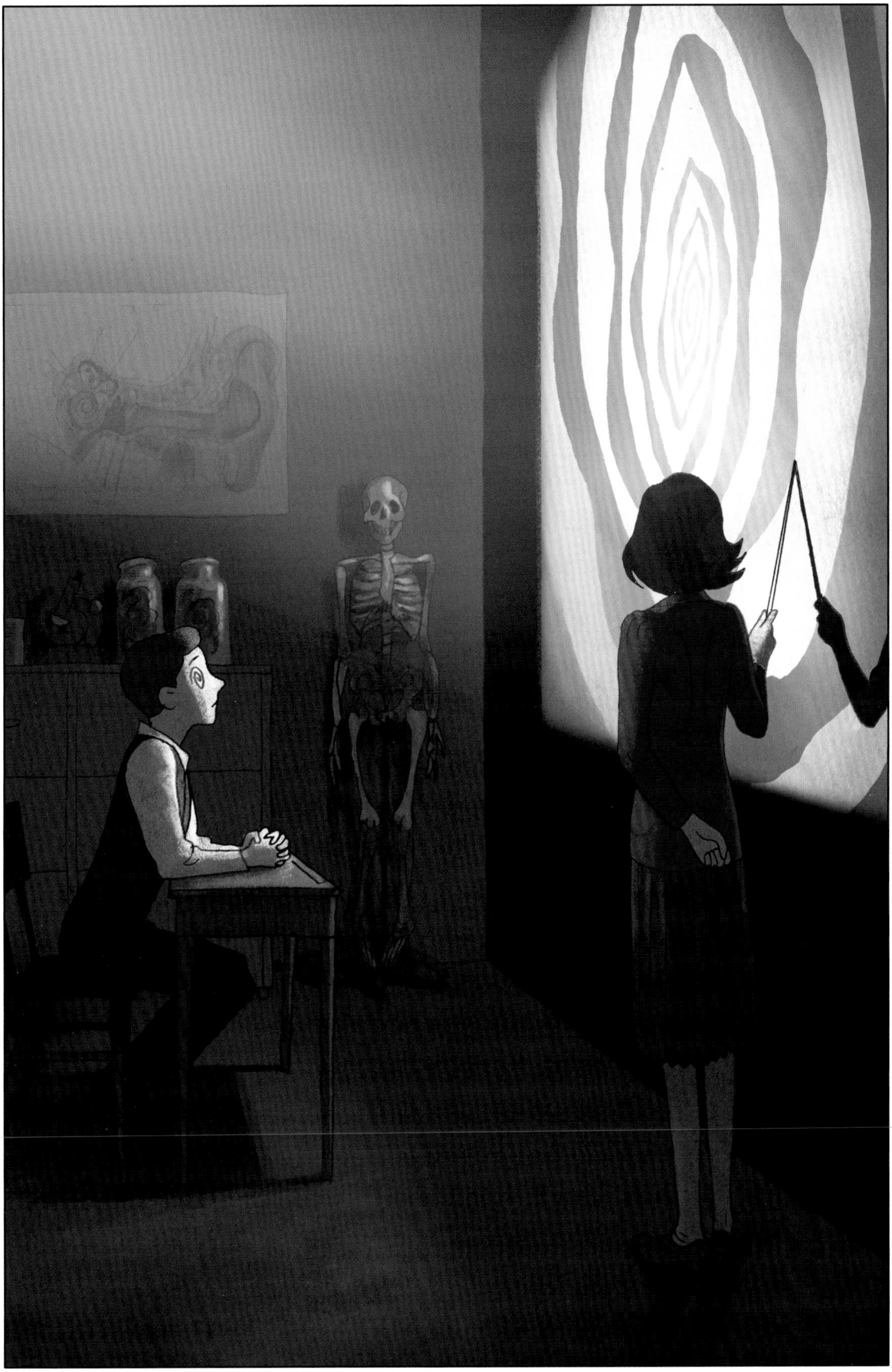

Tuesday, March 28, 1944

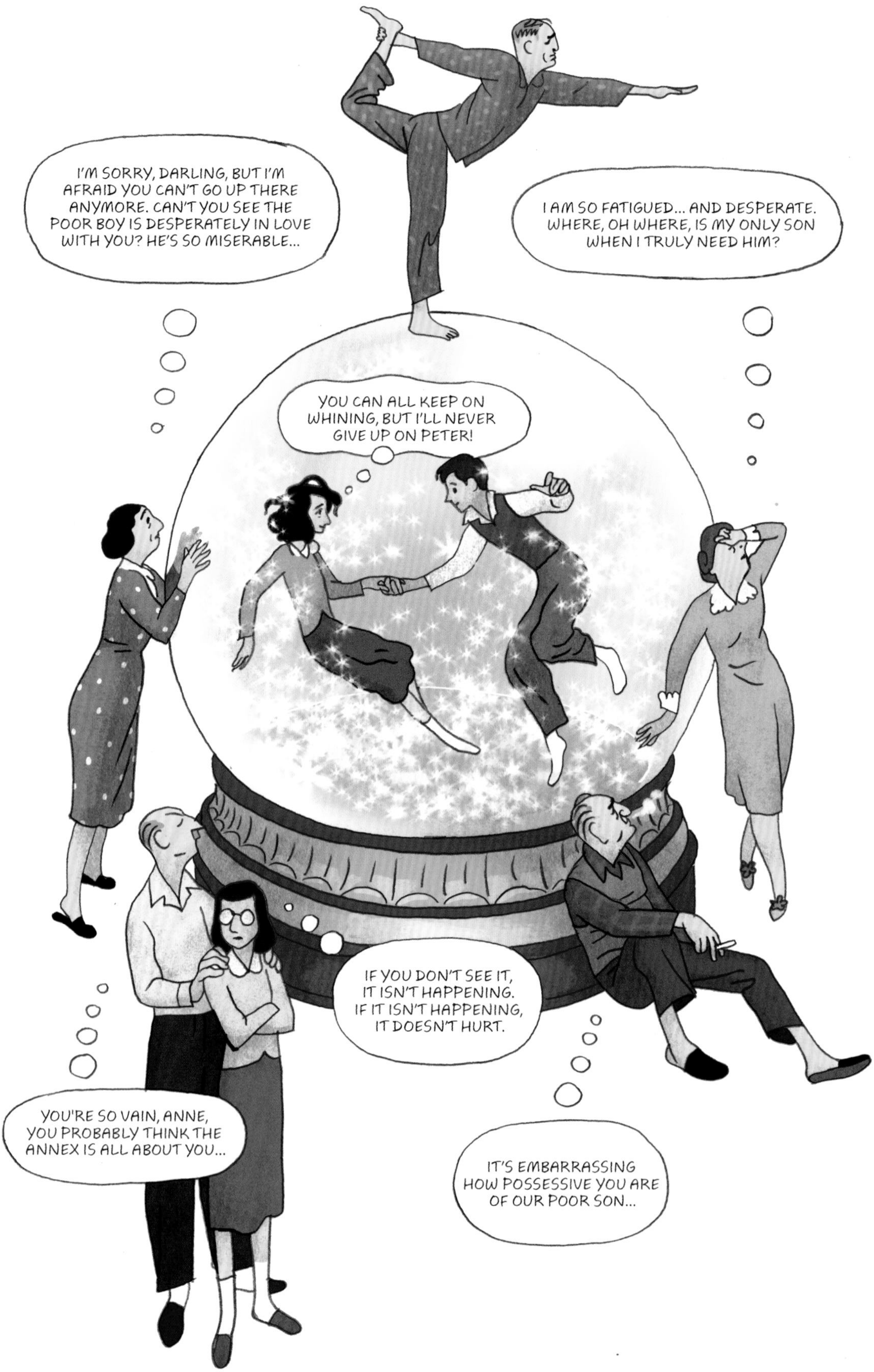
I'M SORRY, DARLING, BUT I'M AFRAID YOU CAN'T GO UP THERE ANYMORE. CAN'T YOU SEE THE POOR BOY IS DESPERATELY IN LOVE WITH YOU? HE'S SO MISERABLE...
I AM SO FATIGUED... AND DESPERATE. WHERE, OH WHERE, IS MY ONLY SON WHEN I TRULY NEED HIM?
YOU CAN ALL KEEP ON WHINING, BUT I'LL NEVER GIVE UP ON PETER!
IF YOU DON'T SEE IT, IT ISN'T HAPPENING. IF IT ISN'T HAPPENING, IT DOESN'T HURT.
YOU'RE SO VAIN, ANNE, YOU PROBABLY THINK THE ANNEX IS ALL ABOUT YOU...
IT'S EMBARRASSING HOW POSSESSIVE YOU ARE OF OUR POOR SON...

I don't understand it: Why are the old people poking their noses into our business again? They have no idea of what draws us together! Fortunately, I'm used to hiding my feelings, so I manage not to show how insane I am about him.

When he lays his head on his arms and closes his eyes, he is still a child.

When he plays with Mouschi, he is so loving.

When he carries potatoes to the attic, he is so strong.

He is so brave when he goes to watch the gunfire...

...or patrols the warehouse to look for thieves.

And when he's so awkward and clumsy, he's helplessly endearing.

Most important, I haven't had many people tell me I'm pretty. Until yesterday:

CAN YOU JUST SMILE FOR ME?

WHY DO YOU ALWAYS ASK ME TO SMILE?

BECAUSE OF THE TWO BEAUTIFUL DIMPLES ON YOUR CHEEKS.

I WAS BORN WITH THEM. THE ONLY MARK OF BEAUTY I POSSESS.

Dear Kitty, Mr. Bolkestein, the Cabinet minister, speaking on the Dutch broadcast from London, said that after the war a collection would be made of diaries and letters dealing with the war. Of course, everyone pounced on my diary. Just imagine how interesting it would be if I were to publish a novel about the Secret Annex.

In the year 3001, archaeologists will expose the biggest sensation of the decade: an entire house from the WWII era.

HEY, BOSS, LOOK WHAT I FOUND!

IT'S NOT A NOVEL, IT'S A DIARY. A DIARY FROM ANCIENT TIMES, BACK WHEN JEWS WERE EXTERMINATED.

They will learn of frightened women who had to run during air raids.

They will learn how buildings can tremble when 350 British planes drop 550 tons of bombs a day.

They won't believe the number of epidemics that raged here in such a short time.

They will be shocked by the price of a single potato.

Doctors can't visit their patients, since their bikes are stolen even during a rescue. Children as young as eight are stealing.

DON'T YOU DARE LEAVE THE HOUSE EVEN FOR A SINGLE SECOND.

On every street corner, stolen goods are for sale.

A week's food ration doesn't last two days. Everyone is extremely weak.

Shoemakers are the new gods. It costs two grams of solid gold to get a sole repaired!

The only good thing is that as the food gets worse and decrees more severe, acts of sabotage against the authorities are taking place on a daily basis.

Monday, April 3, 1944

My dearest Kitty,

Contrary to my usual practice, I'm going to write you a detailed description of the food situation, since it's become a matter of some difficulty and importance, not only here in the Annex, but in all of Holland, all of Europe, and even beyond. In the 21 months we've lived here, we've been through many "food cycles," where we have only one particular dish or vegetable to eat.

December: endive

endive with sand   endive without sand   fried endive   endive soup

January: spinach

rolled spinach   spinach sandwich   spinach mask   spinach fitness

February: meatloaf

meatloaf tartare   meatloaf art   meatloaf pancake   dried meatloaf

March: cucumber

cucumber flambé   cucumber corn   sliced cucumber   sliced cucumber

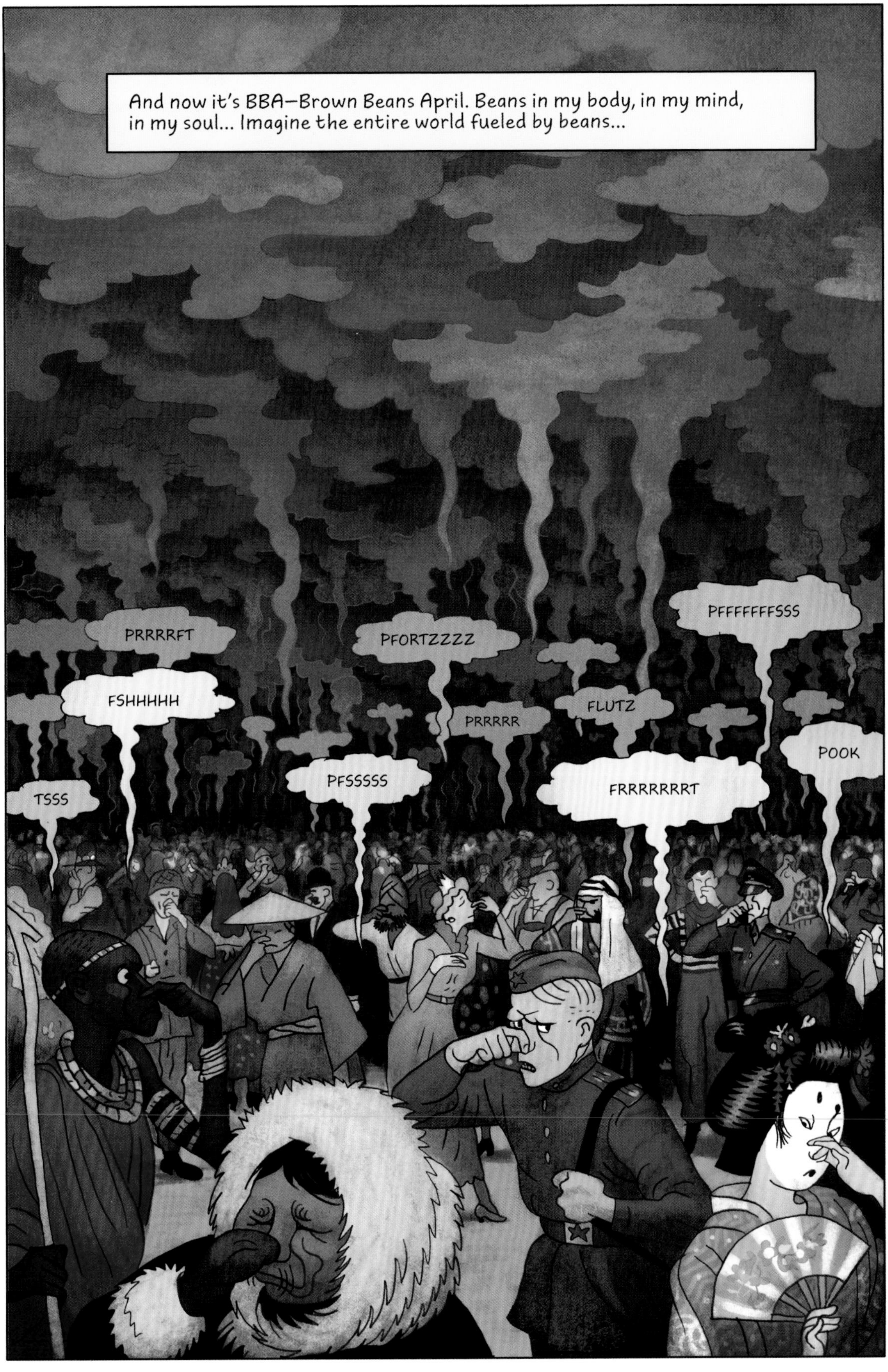
And now it's BBA—Brown Beans April. Beans in my body, in my mind, in my soul... Imagine the entire world fueled by beans...
PRRRRFT
FSHHHHH
TSSS
PFORTZZZZ
PFSSSSS
PRRRRR
PFFFFFFFSSS
FLUTZ
FRRRRRRRT
POOK

Dearest Kitty, We had a lovely Sunday afternoon, listening to a Mozart concert on the radio. Everything was so calm until Peter rushed upstairs to report that there were burglars in the warehouse!

As feared, the police soon arrived and began searching the building. The most terrifying moment was when they were on the other side of the revolving bookcase. When they rattled it, all sounds of breathing stopped, eight hearts pounded. Each and every one of us was absolutely sure we were about to die.

1.

I GO WITH GRACE, IN MY FINAL MOMENTS.

2.

I WISH WE'D BURNED ANNE'S DIARY. IT'S THEIR ONLY EVIDENCE AGAINST US.

3.

I HAVE LIVED AS A LADY, AND I WILL DIE AS A LADY.

4.

MY VERY LAST REQUEST.

5.

DEAR GOD, YOU WERE SO KIND TO ME. THANK YOU.

6.

AT LAST, I AM REWARDED FOR ALWAYS BEING GOOD.

7.

I SHOULD HAVE ASKED HER LAST NIGHT.

8.

IF YOU GO, KITTY, I GO WITH YOU!!

Sunday, April 16, 1944

Dear Kitty, Remember yesterday's date, since it was a red-letter day for me. Isn't it an important day for every girl when she gets her first kiss? Well, then, it's no less important to me.

8:00

SO, IS HE GOING TO MAKE A MOVE BEFORE THE WAR ENDS...?

Last night at eight I was with Peter on his divan, in our usual position.

8:30

IT'S TIME TO MAKE A MOVE.

9:00

MAYBE IT'S JUST ABOUT FRIENDSHIP AFTER ALL.

9:10

I'M SO BORED.

9:15

AHHAAA.

9:30

WELL, PETER, IT'S AFTER NINE. TIME TO GO.

But then...just as I was looking left and he was looking right and we accidentally switched sides, it happened!

Dearest Kitty,

Something extraordinary happened to me yesterday: I realized, for the first time, that there is not only one Anne Frank, but, surprisingly, two Anne Franks. Peter and I were sitting on the divan, as usual, when suddenly the everyday Anne slipped away and the second Anne took her place. The second Anne, who's never overconfident or amusing, but wants only to love and be loved.

The gentle Anne makes infrequent appearances, and she's not about to let herself be shoved out of the door so soon after she's arrived. The second Anne is here to stay!!!

Tuesday, May 2–Friday, May 5, 1944

Dearest Kitty, On Saturday night I asked Peter whether he thinks I should tell Father about us. After we'd discussed it, he said he thought I should. I was glad; it shows he's sensible, and sensitive.

DADDY, I EXPECT YOU'VE GATHERED THAT WHEN PETER AND I ARE TOGETHER WE DON'T EXACTLY SIT AT OPPOSITE ENDS OF THE ROOM.

OH... REALLY?

IS HE IN LOVE WITH YOU?

Then came the restrictions:

DON'T GO UP TO HIM SO OFTEN.

DON'T ENCOURAGE HIM MORE THAN YOU CAN HELP IT.

IT'S ALWAYS THE MAN WHO TAKES THE ACTIVE ROLE, AND IT'S UP TO THE WOMAN TO SET THE LIMITS.

OTHER BOYS AND GIRLS, THEY CAN GO OUTSIDE...

BUT YOU? AND HIM? YOU CAN'T GO AWAY, YOU'RE CAGED.

YOU MIGHT HURT HIM, ANNE, MORE THAN YOU KNOW.

REMEMBER, ANNE, PETER HAS
NO STRENGTH OF CHARACTER.

HE CAN EASILY BE INFLUENCED
TO DO GOOD.

BUT HE CAN DO BAD THINGS
AS WELL.

Father's unhappy with me. After our talk on Sunday he thought I'd stop going upstairs every evening. He won't have any of that "necking" going on. I can't stand that word. Talking about it was bad enough—why does he have to make me feel bad too! I'll have a word with him today. Margot gave me some good advice. Here's more or less what I'd like to say:

I think you expect an explanation from me, Father, so I'll give you one.

You're disappointed in me, you expected more restraint from me, you no doubt want me to act the way a fourteen-year-old is supposed to. But that's where you're wrong!

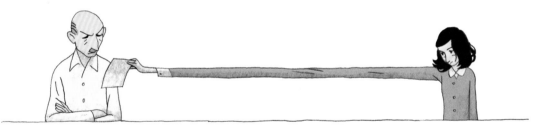

Since we've been here, from July 1942 until a few weeks ago, I haven't had an easy time. If only you knew how much I used to cry at night, how unhappy and despondent I was, how lonely I felt, you'd understand my wanting to go upstairs! I've now reached the point where I don't need the support of Mother or anyone else. I know I'm an independent person, and I don't feel I need to account to you for my actions. I'm only telling you this because I don't want you to think I'm doing things behind your back. But there's only one person I'm accountable to, and that's me. When I was having problems, everyone—and that includes you—closed their eyes and ears and didn't help me. On the contrary, all I ever got were admonitions not to be so noisy. I was noisy only to keep myself from being miserable all the time. Now that it's over, now that I know the battle has been won, I'm independent, in both body and mind, now I want to go my own way, to follow the path that seems right to me. Don't think of me as a fourteen-year-old, since all these troubles have made me older; I won't regret my actions, I'll behave the way I think I should!

Yours,
Anne

Dearest Kitty, As you can no doubt imagine, we often say in despair, What's the point of the war? Why, oh, why can't people live together peacefully? Why all this destruction?

Why is England manufacturing bigger and better airplanes and bombs...

...and at the same time churning out new houses for reconstruction?

Why are millions spent on the war each day...

...while not a penny is available for medical science?

Why do people have to starve...

...when mountains of food are rotting away in other parts of the world?

There's a destructive urge in people, the urge to rage, murder, and kill. And until all of humanity, without exception, undergoes a metamorphosis, wars will continue to be waged, and everything that has been carefully built up, cultivated, and grown will be cut down and destroyed, only to start all over again!

I've often been down in the dumps, but never desperate. I look upon our life in hiding as an interesting adventure, full of danger and romance, and every privation as an amusing addition to my diary. I've made up my mind to lead a different life from other girls, and not to become an ordinary housewife later on. What I'm experiencing here is a good beginning to an interesting life, and that's the reason—the only reason—why I have to laugh at the humorous side of the most dangerous moments.

Dearest Kitty, Have I ever told you anything about our family? I don't think I have, so let me begin. Father was born in Frankfurt am Main to very wealthy parents:

PAPA, I'M AFRAID IT'S TOO HEAVY FOR ME.

OF COURSE IT IS, IT'S PURE GOLD!

In his youth, Father led the life of a rich man's son.

THE PINK CHAMPAGNE IS A 1900 VINTAGE. BOTTOMS UP!

WHICH ONE OF YOU IS GOING TO BE MRS. FRANK?

Mother also came from a fairly well-off family. She used to attend private balls with 250 guests every weekend.

But it was all lost during the Great War, when Father's bank went bankrupt.

Personally, I'm not so set on a bourgeois life, but I still have visions of parties and gorgeous dresses.

Talking of money, Miep told us about her cousin's engagement party, which she went to on Saturday. The cousin's parents are rich, and the groom's are even richer. Miep made our mouths water telling about the food that was served. We had nothing but two spoonfuls of porridge.

VEGETABLE SOUP WITH MEATBALLS, MEAT ROLLS, GATEAU, CHEESE ROLLS, HORS D'OEUVRES MADE WITH EGGS AND ROAST BEEF.

Miep drank ten schnapps and smoked three cigarettes—could this be our temperance advocate? If Miep drank all those, I wonder how many her spouse managed to toss down?

I tell you, we were practically pulling the words right out of her mouth. We were gathered around her as if we'd never in all our lives heard of delicious food or elegant people! If Miep had taken us along to the party, there wouldn't have been any rolls left over for the other guests. If we'd been there, we'd have snatched up everything in sight, including the furniture. The world is a crazy place!

Yours, Anne M. Frank

Thursday, May 11, 1944

Dearest Kitty, I am terribly busy at the moment, and as strange as it may sound, I don't have enough time to get through my pile of work.

This week: finished reading 250 pages of Galileo Galilei.

Next week: second part of Galileo's biography (240 pages).

This week: finished first volume of the biography of Charles V.

Next week: work out the many genealogical charts of Charles V.

Finished studying the Seven Years' War.

Next week: the Nine Years' War.

Learn 50 Greek words by heart.

Learn 50 French words by heart.

My Greeks—Theseus, Oedipus, Orpheus, Jason, and Hercules—needed some attention.

Next week, my beloved movie stars: who won which awards and when.

And now something else. You've known for a long time that my greatest wish is to be a journalist and, later on, a famous writer. We'll have to wait and see if these grand illusions (or delusions!) will ever come true, but till now I've had no lack of topics. In any case, after the war I'd like to publish a book called <u>The Secret Annex</u>.

Meanwhile, I practice with short stories, and I recently finished one, "Cady's Life."

Cady is still in a sanatorium, recovering from the departure of Hans.

When she gets out of the sanatorium she learns that Hans has become a Nazi.

Cady has to break up with Hans again.

In order to recover, she studies nursing.

Years later, Cady meets Hans by chance, at Lake Como.

Cady marries a well-to-do man named Simon. She grows to love him, but not as much as Hans. Hans is always in the back of her mind.

P.S. "Cady" is not just sentimental nonsense, it's based on the story of Father's life! He married the first woman he met after the love of his life left him.

My dearest Kitty, This is D-Day, the BBC announced at 12. "This is the day."
The invasion has begun!

Eleven thousand planes are shuttling back and forth or standing by to land troops and
bombs behind enemy lines. The French coast was bombarded with five thousand five
hundred tons of bombs during the night. Four thousand landing craft and small boats
are continually arriving in the area between Cherbourg and Le Havre. British and
American troops are already engaged in heavy combat. Dummies made of straw and
rubber were dropped from the air behind German lines, and they exploded the minute
they hit the ground. Many paratroopers, their faces blackened so they couldn't be seen
in the dark, landed as well. Oh, Kitty, the best part about the invasion is that I have
the feeling that friends are on the way. Those awful Germans have oppressed and
threatened us for so long that the thought of friends and salvation means everything
to us! Now it's not just the Jews, but Holland and all of occupied Europe.

Maybe, Margot says, I can even go back to school in September or October.

Yours, Anne M. Frank

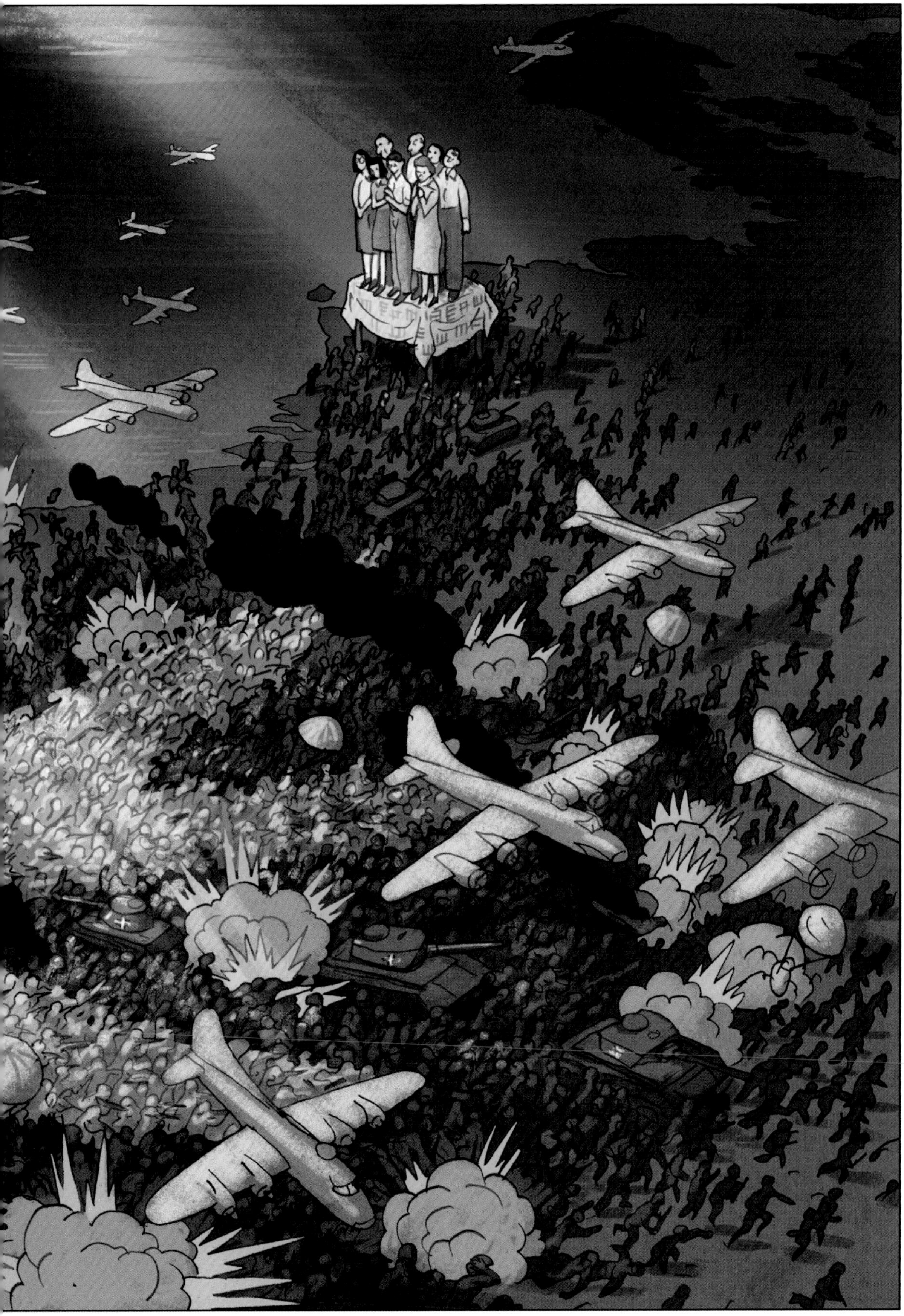

Dearest Kitty, The British have finally rolled up their sleeves and got down to work. Those who keep claiming they don't want to be occupied by the British don't realize how unfair they're being. Their line of reasoning boils down to this: Britain must fight, struggle, and sacrifice its sons to liberate Holland and the other occupied countries. After that the British shouldn't remain in Holland: they should offer their most abject apologies to all the occupied countries, restore the Dutch East Indies to its rightful owner, and then return, weakened and impoverished, to Britain. What a bunch of idiots. All those Dutch people who still look down on the British, scoff at Britain and its government of aging lords, call them cowards, yet hate the Germans, should be given a good shaking, the way you'd plump up a pillow. Maybe that would straighten out their jumbled brains!

One of the many questions that have often bothered me is why women have been, and still are, thought to be so inferior to men. It's easy to say it's unfair, but that's not enough for me; I'd really like to know the reason for this great injustice.

GIRLS, YOU WANT SOME FOOD?

NO THANKS, WE'RE HAPPY JUST FEEDING YOU.

Men presumably dominated women from the very beginning because of their greater physical strength. Women silently went along with this, which was stupid.

Soldiers and war heroes are honored and commemorated, explorers are granted immortal fame, martyrs are revered...

But how many people look upon women too as soldiers? Women, who struggle and suffer pain to ensure the continuation of the human race, make much tougher and more courageous soldiers than all those big-mouthed freedom-fighting heroes put together. It's easy for men to talk—they don't and never will have to bear the woes that women do!

Fortunately, education, work, and progress have opened women's eyes. In many countries they've been granted equal rights; many people, mainly women but also men, now realize how wrong it was to tolerate this state of affairs for so long. Modern women want the right to be completely independent!

Friday, June 16, 1944

Dearest Kitty, New problems: Madame van D. is at her wits' end. She's talking about:

Getting shot

Being hanged

Committing suicide

Being jealous

Offended...

...quarrels, curses, cries, feels sorry for herself, and starts all over again.

And she makes everyone feel even worse than they usually do.

Thursday, July 6, 1944

My blood runs cold when Peter talks about becoming a criminal or a speculator. I have the feeling he's afraid of his own weakness, but he's not the only one.

IF ONLY I HAD YOUR PLUCK AND YOUR STRENGTH!

IF ONLY I HAD YOUR DRIVE!

IF ONLY, IF ONLY... WHAT WOULD YOU DO THEN?

UMMMM... PROBABLY NOTHING

OH, ANNE, I'M SO WEAK.

IF YOU KNOW YOU'RE WEAK, WHY NOT FIGHT IT?

BECAUSE IT'S MUCH EASIER NOT TO.

Peter's beginning to lean on me and I don't want that, not under any circumstances. I've been drifting around at sea, have spent days searching for an effective antidote to that terrible word "easy." How can I make it clear to him that, while it may seem easy and wonderful, it will drag him down to the depths, to a place where he'll no longer find friends, support, or beauty, so far down that he may never rise to the surface again?

Dearest Kitty,

We've received a book from the library with the challenging title <u>What Do You Think of the Modern Young Girl?</u>

I'd like to discuss this subject today.

The writer criticizes "today's youth" from head to toe, though without dismissing them all as "hopeless cases." On the contrary, she believes they have it within their power to build a bigger, better, and more beautiful world, but that they occupy themselves with superficial things, without giving a thought to true beauty.

In some passages I had the strong feeling that the writer was directing her disapproval at me, which is why I finally want to bare my soul to you and defend myself against this attack.

I have one outstanding character trait that must be obvious to anyone who's known me for any length of time: I have a great deal of self-knowledge. In everything I do, I can watch myself as if I were a stranger. I can stand across from the everyday Anne and, without being biased or making excuses, watch what she's doing, both the good and the bad. This self-awareness never leaves me, and every time I open my mouth, I think, "You should have said that differently" or "That's fine the way it is." I condemn myself in so many ways that I'm beginning to realize the truth of Father's adage: "Every child has to raise itself." Parents can only advise their children or point them in the right direction. Ultimately, people shape their own characters. In addition, I face life with an extraordinary amount of courage. I feel so strong and capable of bearing burdens, so young and free! When I first realized this, I was glad, because it means I can more easily withstand the blows life has in store.

Why didn't Father support me in my struggle? Why did he fall short when he tried to offer me a helping hand? The answer is: he used the wrong methods. He always talked to me as if I were a child going through a difficult phase. It sounds crazy, since Father's the only one who's given me a sense of confidence and made me feel as if I'm a sensible person. But he overlooked one thing: he failed to see that this struggle to triumph over my difficulties was more important to me than anything else.

Still, this hasn't been my greatest disappointment. No, I think about Peter much more than I do about Father. I know very well that he was my conquest, and not the other way around. I created an image of him in my mind, pictured him as a quiet, sweet, sensitive boy badly in need of friendship and love! I needed to pour out my heart to a living person. I wanted a friend who would help me find my way again. I accomplished what I set out to do and drew him, slowly but surely, toward me. When I finally got him to be my friend, it automatically developed into an intimacy that, when I think about it now, seems outrageous. It was a mistake to use intimacy to get closer to him, because in doing so, I ruled out other forms of friendship. He longs to be loved, and I can see he's beginning to like me more with each passing day. I forced Peter, more than he realizes, to get close to me, and now he's holding on for dear life. I honestly don't see any effective way of shaking him off and getting him back on his own two feet. I soon realized he could never be a kindred spirit, but still tried to help him break out of his narrow world and expand his youthful horizons.

"Deep down, the young are lonelier than the old." I read this in a book somewhere and it's stuck in my mind. As far as I can tell, it's true. So if you're wondering whether it's harder for the adults here than for the children, the answer is no, it's certainly not. Older people have an opinion about everything and are sure of themselves and their actions. It's twice as hard for us young people to hold on to our opinions at a time when ideals are being shattered and destroyed, when the worst side of human nature predominates, when everyone has come to doubt truth, justice, and God.

Anyone who claims that the old people have a more difficult time in the Annex doesn't realize that the problems have a far greater impact on us. We're much too young to deal with these problems, but they keep thrusting themselves on us until, finally, we're forced to think up a solution, though most of the time our solutions crumble when faced with the facts. It's difficult in times like these: ideals, dreams, and cherished hopes rise within us, only to be crushed by grim reality. It's a wonder I haven't abandoned all my ideals, they seem so absurd and impractical. Yet I cling to them because I still believe, in spite of everything, that people are truly good at heart.

It's utterly impossible for me to build my life on a foundation of chaos, suffering, and death. I see the world being slowly transformed into a wilderness, I hear the approaching thunder that, one day, will destroy us too, I feel the suffering of millions. And yet, when I look up at the sky, I somehow feel that everything will change for the better, that this cruelty too will end, that peace and tranquility will return once more. In the meantime, I must hold on to my ideals.

Perhaps the day will come when I'll be able to realize them!

Yours, Anne M. Frank

Friday, July 21, 1944

Dearest Kitty, I'm finally getting optimistic. Now, at last, things are going well! They really are! Great news! An assassination attempt has been made on Hitler's life.

MEIN FÜHRER, I AM SORRY BUT I MUST GO NOW, MY WIFE IS DEPRESSED AT HOME.

HE FORGOT HIS VALISE— I'LL RUN AFTER HIM.

DON'T BOTHER, HIS WIFE WILL KILL HIM ANYWAY.

WAS IT A JEW?

NO, MEIN FÜHRER.

A COMMUNIST?

NO, MEIN FÜHRER.

SO?

IT WAS ONE OF US.

Hitler escaped, unfortunately, with only a few minor burns and scratches. A number of the officers and generals who were nearby were killed or wounded. The head of the conspiracy has been shot. This is the best proof we've had so far that many officers and generals are fed up with the war and would like to see Hitler sink into a bottomless pit.

They plan to establish a military dictatorship, make peace with the Allies...

...rearm themselves secretly...

...and after a few decades, start a new war.

Now that the Führer's order is out, imagine this: Little Fritz is fleeing the Russian army, his feet hurt from running.

Fritz grabs his rifle.

Eventually, every time an officer sees a soldier or gives an order, he'll be practically wetting his pants, because the soldiers have more say-so than he does. Germans killing Germans: the Allies' dream.

Tuesday, August 1, 1944

Dearest Kitty,

"A bundle of contradictions" was the end of my previous letter and is the beginning of this one. Can you please tell me exactly what "a bundle of contradictions" is? What does "contradiction" mean? Like so many words, it can be interpreted in two ways: a contradiction imposed from without and one imposed from within. The former means not accepting other people's opinions, always knowing best, having the last word; in short, all those unpleasant traits for which I'm known. The latter, for which I'm not known, is my own secret. As I've told you many times, I'm split in two. One side contains my exuberant cheerfulness, my flippancy, my joy in life, and, above all, my ability to appreciate the lighter side of things. By that I mean not finding anything wrong with flirtations, a kiss, an embrace, a saucy joke. Oh, I can be an amusing clown for an afternoon, but after that everyone's had enough of me to last a month.

Actually, I'm what a romantic film is to a profound thinker—a mere diversion, a comic interlude, something that is soon forgotten: not bad, but not particularly good either... I'm afraid that people who know me as I usually am will discover I have another side, a better and finer side. I'm afraid they'll mock me, think I'm ridiculous and sentimental and not take me seriously. So the nice Anne is never seen in company. She's never made a single appearance, though she almost always takes the stage when I'm alone. I know exactly how I'd like to be, how I am... on the inside. But unfortunately I'm only like that with myself. And perhaps that's why—no, I'm sure that's the reason why—I think of myself as happy on the inside and other people think I'm happy on the outside. The happy-go-lucky Anne laughs, gives a flippant reply, shrugs her shoulders, and pretends she couldn't care less. The quiet Anne reacts in just the opposite way. If I'm being completely honest, I'll have to admit that it does matter to me, that I'm trying very hard to change myself, but that I'm always up against a more powerful enemy. A voice within me is sobbing, "You see, that's what's become of you. You're surrounded by negative opinions, dismayed looks, and mocking faces, people who dislike you, and all because you don't listen to the advice of your own better half." Believe me, I'd like to listen, but it doesn't work, because if I'm quiet and serious, everyone thinks I'm putting on a new act and I have to save myself with a joke, and then I'm not even talking about my own family, who assume I must be ill, stuff me with aspirins and sedatives, feel my neck and forehead to see if I have a temperature, ask about my bowel movements, and berate me for being in a bad mood, until I just can't keep it up anymore, because when everybody starts hovering over me, I get cross, then sad, and finally end up turning my heart inside out, the bad part on the outside and the good part on the inside, and keep trying to find a way to become what I'd like to be and what I could be if... if only there were no other people in the world.

Yours, Anne M. Frank

Anne's diary ends here.

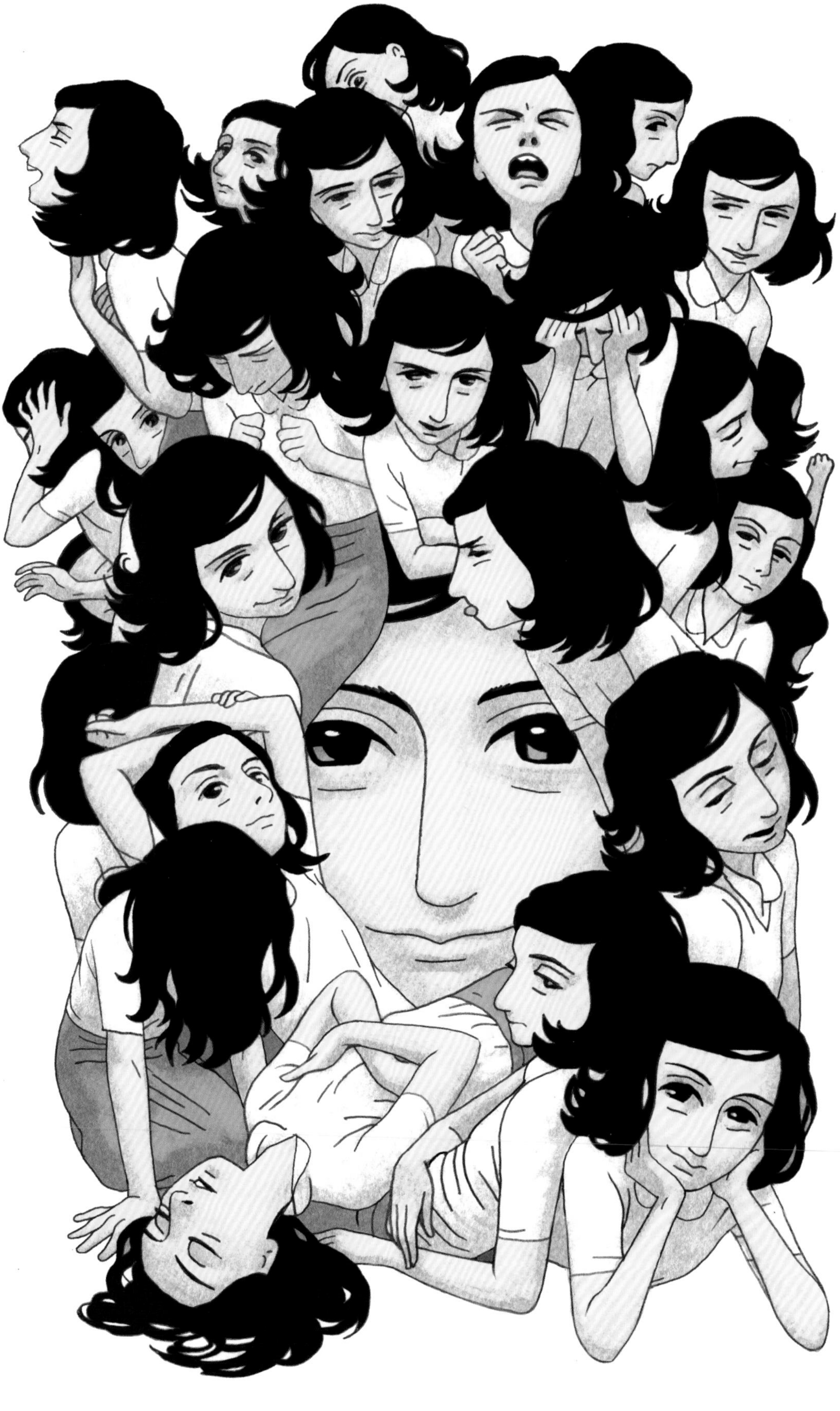

Afterword

On the morning of August 4, 1944, sometime between 10:00 and 10:30 a.m., a car pulled up at 263 Prinsengracht. Several figures emerged: an SS sergeant, Karl Josef Silberbauer, in full uniform, and at least three Dutch members of the Security Police, armed but in civilian clothes. Someone must have tipped them off.

They arrested the eight people hiding in the Annex, as well as two of their helpers, Victor Kugler and Johannes (Jo) Kleiman—though not Miep Gies and Elisabeth (Bep) Voskuijl—and took all the valuables and cash they could find in the Annex.

After the arrest, Kugler and Kleiman were taken to a prison in Amsterdam. On September 11, 1944, they were transferred, without benefit of a trial, to a camp in Amersfoort (Holland). Kleiman, because of his poor health, was released on September 18, 1944. He remained in Amsterdam until his death in 1959.

Kugler managed to escape his imprisonment on March 28, 1945, when he and his fellow prisoners were being sent to Germany as forced laborers. He immigrated to Canada in 1955 and died in Toronto in 1981.

Elisabeth (Bep) Voskuijl Wijk died in Amsterdam in 1983.

Miep Santrouschitz Gies died on January 11, 2010, in the Netherlands at the age of one hundred; her husband, Jan, died in 1993.

Upon their arrest, the eight residents of the Annex were first taken to a prison in Amsterdam and then transferred to Westerbork, the transit camp for Jews in the north of Holland. They were deported on September 3, 1944, in the last transport to leave Westerbork, and arrived three days later in Auschwitz (Poland).

Hermann van Pels (van Daan) was, according to the testimony of Otto Frank, gassed to death in Auschwitz in October or November 1944, shortly before the gas chambers were dismantled.

Auguste van Pels (Petronella van Daan) was transported from Auschwitz to Bergen-Belsen, from there to Buchenwald, then to Theresienstadt on April 9, 1945, and apparently to another concentration camp after that. It is certain that she did not survive, though the date of her death is unknown.

Peter van Pels (van Daan) was forced to take part in the January 16, 1945, death march from Auschwitz to Mauthausen (Austria), where he died on May 5, 1945, three days before the camp was liberated.

Fritz Pfeffer (Albert Dussel) died on December 20, 1944, in the Neuengamme concentration camp, where he had been transferred from either Buchenwald or Sachsenhausen.

Edith Frank died in Auschwitz-Birkenau on January 6, 1945, from hunger and exhaustion.

Margot and Anne Frank were transported from Auschwitz at the end of October and taken to Bergen-Belsen, a concentration camp near Hannover (Germany). The typhus epidemic that broke out in the winter of 1944–45, as a result of the horrendous hygiene conditions, killed thousands of prisoners, including Margot and, a few days later, Anne. She must have died in late February or early March. The bodies of both girls were probably dumped in Bergen-Belsen's mass graves. The camp was liberated by British troops on April 12, 1945.

Otto Frank was the only one of the eight to survive the concentration camps. After Auschwitz was liberated by Russian troops, he was repatriated to Amsterdam by way of Odessa and Marseilles. He arrived in Amsterdam on June 3, 1945, and stayed there until 1953, when he moved to Basel (Switzerland), where his sister with her family, his mother, and later his brother lived. He married Elfriede Markovits Geiringer, originally from Vienna, who had survived Auschwitz and lost a husband and son in Mauthausen. Otto Frank pursued the worldwide publication of the diary and used all proceeds for charitable and educational purposes. In 1963 he founded the Anne Frank Fonds Basel (AFF). It was the only organization he established, designated as his universal heir and chaired by Anne Frank's cousin, Buddy Elias, from 1996 until his death in 2015. As owner of the copyrights of the family archives, the AFF has the responsibility to publish the Diary of Anne Frank. To this day the AFF carries on in this tradition, fulfilling Otto Frank's legacy. Until his death on August 19, 1980, Otto Frank continued to live in Birsfelden, outside Basel, where he devoted himself to sharing the message of his daughter's diary with people all over the world. He and his wife are buried in Birsfelden.

Adapter's Note

In his book *The End of the Holocaust,* the eminent historian Alvin Rosenfeld contends that "more people are probably familiar with the Nazi era through the figure of Anne Frank than through any other figure of that period with the possible exception of Adolf Hitler himself." So, when the Anne Frank Fonds in Basel contacted me five years ago, proposing that I write and direct an animated film for children based on Anne's diary, as well as edit the diary into a graphic adaptation, I had grave reservations. In particular the idea of the graphic adaptation gave me pause. Rereading Anne's diary as an adult and a parent to adolescent children was both stunning and enchanting. It was astounding to me that a thirteen-year-old girl had been able to take such a mature, lyrical look at the world and translate that into concise, probing entries brimming with compassion and humor, and with a degree of self-awareness that I have rarely encountered in the adult world, much less among children. The text is iconic. How could I "edit" the book? The project also posed a significant challenge: if we were to illustrate the entire text in a graphic rendition it would require the better part of a decade and likely be 3,500 pages long. The trickiest task, then, would be to retain only a portion of Anne's original diary while still being faithful to the entire work.

Not all the diary entries could be included and many would need to be amalgamated. Anne made four diary entries in the first eight days, which in the graphic adaptation became one ten-page entry, describing her life as a popular girl admired by the boys in her class, as well as introducing readers to the deteriorating conditions of Jews, and of the Franks in particular, because of the increasingly draconian Nazi laws.

Another example: Anne's repeated—and unresolved—comparisons throughout the diary of her "problematic" self with her "perfect" sister, Margot, we chose to encapsulate on a single graphic page that visualizes the contrasts.

We made no attempt to guess in what manner Anne might have drawn her diary if she had been an artist instead of a writer. We did, however, try to visually interpret and preserve her powerful sense of humor, her sarcasm (especially when it comes to Mrs. van Daan, a character that both the illustrator, David Polonsky, and I were particularly fond of), and her obsessive preoccupation with food (the graphic adaptation repeatedly dwells on coping with the endless hunger in hiding).

For Anne's periods of depression and despair, we chose to depict them as either fantastical scenes (such as Jews rebuilding the pyramids under the Nazi whip) or as dreams.

As the diary progresses, Anne's talents as a writer grow ever more impressive, and by 1944, when she falls desperately in love with Peter, her craft has evolved from tentative to wise-beyond-her-years. It seemed intolerable to forgo these later entries in favor of illustrations, and so we chose to reproduce long passages in their entirety, unillustrated.

We have undertaken this project with the intent to remain true to Anne Frank's memory and legacy and have weighed our options with care. On behalf of David Polonsky and myself, I wish to declare that we are sensitive to and aware of the liberties we have taken, and that our goal was always foremost to honor and preserve the spirit of Anne Frank in each and every frame. David and I also wish to thank Yoni Goodman for the storyboards, Yael Nahlieli for production assistance, Hila Noam for the coloring, Jessica Cohen for the final editing of the text, and, especially, Yves Kugelmann from the Anne Frank Fonds, without whom this book would never have been published.

—Ari Folman

A Note About the Author

ANNE FRANK was born in 1929 in Frankfurt, Germany. Her family moved to Amsterdam in 1933, and she died in the Bergen-Belsen concentration camp in 1945. Her diary, published as *The Diary of a Young Girl,* which documents her life in hiding from 1942 to 1944, is one of the world's most widely known books and has been the basis for several plays and films.

A Note About the Adapter

ARI FOLMAN is an Israeli director, screenwriter, and film score composer. He has written for several successful Israeli TV series, including the award-winning *In Therapy* (*Be Tipul*), which was the basis for the HBO series *In Treatment*. He is the director of the Golden Globe–winning and Oscar-nominated *Waltz with Bashir* and *The Congress* and is working on the animated film *Where Is Anne Frank,* which will be released in 2020.

A Note About the Illustrator

DAVID POLONSKY graduated from Bezalel Academy of Arts and Design, Jerusalem, in 1998. David's illustrations have appeared in most of Israel's leading newspapers and magazines. He was the art director and lead artist for *Waltz with Bashir,* an animated documentary feature and an official selection in the 2008 Cannes film festival. He has illustrated a number of children's books, and won the Israel Museum award for children's book illustration in 2004 and 2008. Since 1999 he has taught animation and illustration at the Bezalel Academy of Arts and Design in Israel.